THE LADY BE GOOD

THE LADY BE GOOD

Mystery Bomber of World War II

DENNIS E. McCLENDON

FIRST EDITION
SEVENTH PRINTING

© 1962 by **Dennis E. McClendon**. Epilogue © 1982 by **Dennis McClendon**.
Published by TAB/AERO Books, an imprint of TAB Books.
TAB Books is a division of McGraw-Hill, Inc.

Library of Congress Cataloging-in-Publication Data

McClendon, Dennis E.
    The Lady Be Good.

    1. Lady Be Good (Airplane)   2. World War, 1939-1945—
Aerial operations, American.   I. Title.
[D790.M25   1987]   940.54′4973   87-1454
ISBN 0-8306-8624-X (pbk.)

TAB Books offers software for sale. For information and a catalog, please contact
TAB Software Department, Blue Ridge Summit, PA 17294-0850.

Questions regarding the content of this book should be addressed to:

Reader Inquiry Branch
TAB Books
Blue Ridge Summit, PA 17294-0850

ACKNOWLEDGMENTS

A factual book is never written alone, and this one is no exception. I am indebted to more than a score of generous persons for their unstinted help, over a period of more than two years, in searching out the facts needed to solve this perplexing mystery.

My deepest gratitude goes to Wilbur J. Nigh, archivist, Federal Records Center, Alexandria, Virginia, for his aid and advice in obtaining the original 376th Bomb Group records upon which this story is based; Ebert C. Smith, historian, Office of Information, Wright-Patterson Air Force Base, Ohio, for his persistent efforts in tracking down the detailed history of the two B-24 aircraft involved; the staff of the Historical Division, Research Studies Institute, Air University, Maxwell Air Force Base, Alabama, for digging through hundreds of mission reports of the 376th Bomb Group and isolating all those pertaining to the April 4, 1943, attack on Naples harbor; John C. Vyn, of Highland Park, Illinois (a cousin of the *Lady Be Good*'s navigator, who is preparing a thesis in modern history on the *Lady Be Good*), for his generous loan of dozens of letters, newspaper clippings, photographs and military reports; Senior Master Sergeant Hal Bamford, of the USAF *Airman* magazine staff, for his help in reconstructing the low-level Ploesti, Romania, raid of August 1, 1943; Robert E. Costello, executive producer of the Armstrong Circle Theater, for the loan of photographs and the exchange of information; to the following members of the wartime 376th Bomb Group for personal accounts of missions, personal photographs, and for translating isolated facts into the whole fabric of specific events: Lieutenant Colonel Paul J. Fallon, Eglin Air Force Base, Florida; Lieutenant Colonel Martin J. Walsh, Office of Assistant Chief of Staff, Reserve Affairs Headquarters, USAF; Edwin L. Gluck, Pittsburgh, Pennsylvania; Captain Jack Preble (USAF, Retired), Steubenville, Ohio; Captain Millard B. Kesler, USAFR, Hillsboro, Ohio; and Captain Myron T. Holmes, Plattsburgh Air Force Base, New York; Lieutenant Colonel Sidney Williams, Chief of the U. S. Army Magazines and Books Branch, for specific facts concerning casualty reports on the *Lady Be Good*'s crewmen; Mr. T. Bickford, Libyan Area Superintendent for the British Petroleum Company, for his tremendously helpful account of the finding of the *Lady*

Be Good and for his advice on the geologic structure of
Libya and the means by which oil is discovered there;
Lieutenant Colonel Kenneth Puttkamer, Chief, Office
of Information and Civil Affairs, Wheelus Air Base,
Libya, and his assistant, Walt C. Wandell, for a veritable flood of information, advice, photographs and
other assistance; my wife, Vivian McClendon, for the
maps in this text and for many readings and corrections
of various drafts of this story; Major Jim Sunderman,
Chief of the Air Force Book Program, for his en-
couragement; and to Moncel A. Monts, now retired
from his long tenure as Chief of the Air Force News
Branch, Department of Defense, for allowing me a
week, as one of his press officers, to dig out the original
information in the Department of Defense fact sheet
of July 27, 1959, which first officially set the record
straight on the *Lady Be Good*'s last flight.

FOREWORD

In May 1959 word was flashed to the world of a mysterious American bomber that had apparently landed by itself in the trackless wastes of the Libyan Sahara Desert.

The bomber, a heavy four-engined B-24 Liberator of World War II vintage, was damaged very little—in itself a minor miracle. But that was not the major mystery: There were no traces of the bomber's crew.

Had the B-24 been found in the year 2000 instead of 1959, it is unlikely that anyone could have discovered what brought about this strange occurrence. Even in 1959 the mystery took more than two years to fathom. And if the bomber had gone undiscovered for another generation—as well it might have—the men able to decipher the B-24 and its crew from history would probably have been dead.

The fascinating, courageous and almost futile story of the men who flew the mystery bomber might never have been known but for man's never-ending search for new sources of oil.

Illustrations will be found following page 96

THE LADY BE GOOD

1

A GEOLOGIST OF solid Scots ancestry peered through the window of his aircraft, sweeping the desert floor beneath with eyes as efficient as radar antennae. Momentarily his vision focused.

Ronald G. MacLean was searching the desert for traces of oil-bearing rock strata. When his side-sweeps stopped, the object which usually riveted his attention would be a telltale rock formation.

But it was no rock that caught his practiced eye that blistering 110-degree afternoon of November 9, 1958. What he saw looked like another airplane. That in itself was strange—385 miles dead south of Tobruk. Airplanes rarely flew over the southeast Libyan Desert.

MacLean's flight was an exception. He and S. V. Sykes, a fellow geologist, were making an aerial reconnaissance from a small airstrip in the Cufra Oases, 135

miles to the south. Their purpose in flying over the
region was one of the few with which sane men would
even approach this barren Sahara Desert fringe.

The object on the sand below was definitely another
airplane. At a nod from MacLean, the pilot flew closer
and circled for a better look. What they saw was obviously a large military plane—an old World War II
heavy bomber, by the looks of it; its wing showed a
distinct American white star set in a blue circle. Mac-
Lean had seen that insignia before. The bomber was
painted pink, almost the color of parts of the desert at
times. It must have been damaged while attempting a
crash landing.

Methodically MacLean had his pilot mark the approximate location on his map, for possible future reference. It was not possible to pinpoint anything from
the air more accurately than 25 miles or so in this
barely mapped region, but any landmark might have
some later use.

The pilot turned back to Cufra, landing on the airstrip at El Giof. Waiting were members of a British
oil-exploration party which had come to the Oases a
month earlier by overland convoy. MacLean and Sykes
had taken advantage of a resupply flight to look over
an area which the party was to explore during the
months ahead.

The group returned to Tripoli the following day.
MacLean and Sykes filed their geological and geograph-
ical data—including a notation about the American

bomber—with their firm, the D'Arcy Exploration Company, Ltd., of Tripoli and Benghazi.

It was odd that this plane had been so far off the beaten track, but there was really no point in making any further report. Anyone who flew over North Africa could see hundreds of wrecked Italian, German, British and American aircraft in the desert.

Burned out British tanks mingled with gutted German Tigers, American Shermans and a wide variety of Italian makes. There were Savoia-Marchetti tri-motored bombers, Luftwaffe JU-87 Stukas, American B-25 Mitchells, British Spitfire and Hurricane fighters, American P-40 Warhawks, British Bristol Blenheims, and German Messerschmitt 109s and Focke-Wulf 190s. Wrecked Junkers 52 air transports were mixed with American C-47s and British Avro Ansons. The litter of motorcycles, gun carriages, artillery shell casings and ration boxes strewed the desert for hundreds of miles along the coast. And in the harbors of the scorched small Libyan and Egyptian seaports, rusting hulks of bombed and torpedoed ships thrust sharply up from shallow waters. This had been a major theater of military operations in the early years of World War II. Bodies were still being found by those who braved the remnant mine fields—bodies of Poles, Germans, Egyptians, Sudanese, Australians, Danes, Canadians, Hungarians, Palestinian Jews, Arabs, Americans, Italians, Indians.

Of Americans alone, there were still many thousands

listed as "missing in action" in Europe and Africa—the
Americans had come last to the area. Many bodies lying
in remote areas might never be found.

So it was not unusual that MacLean and Skyes felt
little excitement on spotting a lone American bomber
in this desert. Nor was it unusual to note it on their
exploration map. Men searching a completely unknown region record everything that may be helpful
as a reference point in the future; and their company
had definite future plans for this area, with its rich pros-
pect of oil. The French had already developed major
fields some hundreds of miles to the west, in the Algerian Sahara; had found so much oil there, in fact,
that it had become commercially profitable to build
pipelines from the desert to Algerian and Tunisian
seaports.

Libya was a poor, underpopulated country, and
could well use these oil revenues. The average per
capita income of its people in 1950 had been a paltry
$35 annually—the lowest in the Middle East. The
desert areas were particularly wretched. In the narrow,
fertile coastal section—a mere 3 per cent of the country's
territory—lived 90 per cent of Libya's million people.

To oil explorers Libya held a look of promise. The
country sat atop a huge layer of limestone, on the average almost 3,000 feet thick. While this ravenously porous rock would not allow water to stay on its surface in
the areas where it was not capped with impervious rock
strata, it did hold water in its layers beneath the surface

—as proved by myriads of oases dotting its aridity. Porous sedimentary rock could also hold oil. This entire country had once been a sea floor—part of the prehistoric Mediterranean Basin—and ancient animal life had settled to the sea bottom as it died there, in persistent layer after layer, rising only a scant inch or so each thousand years. When the land finally emerged from the sea millions of years later, it was nearly certain that the sea-animal remains, trapped beneath the surface among layers of limestone formations, had—over the ages—been transformed into oil.

An exploring geologist's initial task was to fly over a promising area and mark his charts with the locations most likely to contain subsurface dome, anticline or fault structures. Next, other geologists, geophysicists, surveyors and equipment would be sent to explore those areas more intimately. With seismographic detection equipment, the underlying rock strata could be proved out by setting off charges of dynamite and making careful sounding charts. A pattern would soon emerge and likely locations could then be drilled for possible traps of the black gold below. Experts felt certain that the Libyan Desert contained oil, and recommended spending huge sums of money to find it.

Oil might well be the only salvation for modern Libya. The longer a man stayed there, the more deeply he felt the poverty of its people, deplored their present miseries, and marveled at their past glories.

It was a shock to visit the Greek and Roman ruins of

once-flourishing Cyrene—between Benghazi and Tobruk. This was the birthplace of Aristippus, pupil of
Socrates and first of the Cyrenaic philosophers, with
his inviting theory that happiness is more important
than virtue. (But that prudence must govern its pur-
suit "lest the pleasure turn to pain.") This was also the
birthplace of the philosopher-astronomer Eratosthenes,
one of the first to measure the earth's circumference
with passable accuracy.

Once an important center of trade and culture—with
about 100,000 prosperous inhabitants—Cyrene had
been founded more than 2,000 years earlier, in 630
B.C., by the enterprising Greeks who made it a capital
of a region they called Pentapolis. The Romans took
over the colony in 96 B.C. and named the region Cyrenaica, and it continued to flourish. Today Cyrene is
reduced to 500 people who make a living mainly by
showing their grandiose ruins to tourists. The eastern
half of Libya is still called Cyrenaica, and the summer
capital of the nation is located in the Cyrenaican port
city of Benghazi which still has nearly 65,000 people.

Benghazi changed hands five times during World
War II. The entire surrounding area was bitterly con-
tested, first by the British against the Italians, then by
the British against both Italians and Germans, and
finally by the British with American help against Marshal Erwin Rommel's Afrika Korps and his Italian
allies.

The Italians had previously required twenty years—

from 1911 to 1931—to wrest Cyrenaica from its people, and had killed almost a third of the population in the process. After World War II, the United Nations made long-suffering Cyrenaica in the east and Tripolitania in the west into the independent United Kingdom of Libya, the new country formally achieving independence on December 24, 1951. Its nearly 1,000,000 remaining citizens are now approximately one-third Berber origin and two-thirds Negro or mulatto descent. The Negro portion dates from the ancient days when successive waves of European conquerors brought slaves north from Central Africa. Few population groups foreign to the basic Berber and Negro stocks live in Libya today.

Probably the only significant influx of foreigners are the United States Air Force people who operate Wheelus Air Base on the eastern outskirts of Tripoli; the British military forces at El Adem Airport near Tobruk; the polyglot small groups who scavenge the former battlefields for scrap iron, and sweep essential areas free of leftover World War II mines; and the multilingual national groups which operate the foreign oil-exploration concessions with the Libyan Government's permission.

In August, 1958, Gordon Bowerman, a young Englishman who was already an experienced hand in oil exploration, arrived in Libya to work for the D'Arcy Company. After a stint in Tanganyika and several months of close-in assignments, Bowerman—a surveyor by profession—had been assigned to work with the oil-exploration party operating out of El Giof, to chart the ground strata under the plateau marked by Ronald MacLean the previous year. The Cufra party had not yet worked to the north toward Tobruk.

Young Bowerman flew to El Giof in February, 1959. Arriving at the desert oasis, he was pleasantly amazed at the lush date palms, the flourishing vegetable and melon gardens, the beturbaned Berbers—silent and impassive at the wonder of his airplane—and the relative green coolness in the midst of so much far-stretching hot sand. But he had little time to absorb his exotic surroundings of braying camels, of *muezzins* calling the Islamic faithful to prayer, and of nomads cooking contaminating bacteria out of their meager food supply over cheerful, hot fires of burning camel dung.

On hand to meet him were D. J. R. Sheridan, in charge of the D'Arcy party, and A. J. Martin. The two geologists were in from the desert to pick up their new surveyor and return to work the next day. Supplies for the trip were loaded that evening, and in the early morning the party was off.

Operating with a convoy of light Land Rover jeep-like vehicles and a three-ton Bedford truck containing supplies, the three men and their Libyan helpers set out to chart the unmapped plateau area which began some 90 miles due north.

After two long weeks of hot, miserable days in the broken, superheated rock garden, the convoy broke out on the plateau on March 1st. The flat, pebble-and-sand floor was roughly 500 feet above sea level, and was as nearly totally desolate as any place these much-traveled men had seen. Behind them were the last of the rock escarpments—topping 2,300 feet in places—and ahead, for the five miles or so that they could see from their Land Rovers, stretched a level nothing.

Life and death were both tangible on the plateau. Even in the spring the climate was almost beyond endurance. The sun baked down from a mercilessly cloudless sky running daytime temperatures up to 100-120 degrees, while at night the thermometer plunged to near freezing. There was not a single tiny sprig of vegetation to be seen, and fine sand dust permeated everything from nostrils and clothing to food and water. Working conditions were onerous.

The men noticed that even the misguided birds who had flown into the area had been forced to remain. There were jagged carpets of them—dead and mummified—in the fleeting shadows of the rock outcroppings in which they had found momentary respite from the sun. Just as an airplane requires much longer runways to become airborne in extremely hot weather, the birds had evidently required greater wing motion to fly in this thin, torrid air. That need for extra effort had come at a time when they could not expend it; they were already exhausted and they had no water, food, shelter—no way to build up strength. So they had died, and in the searing, dry air had been dehydrated into hardened mummies.

Sheridan, Martin and Bowerman, carefully noting their survey findings on their geological maps, had noticed earlier the MacLean notes about a crashed American bomber on the central southern part of the plateau. As soon as the party began operations in that general area, the men began to keep a sharp lookout. The plane would be difficult to locate from the ground, since they could see no farther than five miles over the plateau floor, and since the marked location map was only approximate at best. Eventually, though, they sighted it.

The mute wreckage of the great, heavy bomber huddled close into the sand—almost as though attempting to avoid detection. Its machine guns pointed menacingly at the newcomers.

The big plane was so little damaged that the men at first thought its crew might have bellied it into the plateau—with a somewhat harder landing than usual. Its fuselage was broken in the middle, and one of the four engines was knocked loose from the wing. But other than that, it seemed in extremely good condition. It looked as though a crew could quite easily have survived its crash landing.

Entering through a break in the fuselage, the men agreed that the interior had a haunted appearance. Items of the crew's equipment were all about, flight logs were there, ammunition still hung ready in feed belts by the outpointing machine guns. There were several kinds of supplies—the kind that men in the desert would desperately need—but no evidence that the interior had been touched after the plane had landed. Fantastic though it seemed to the men, heat baked as they were and suspicious of illusions, it looked as though the bomber had landed entirely by itself.

In the immediate vicinity there was not a single sign of the aircrew—dead or otherwise. There were no unopened or opened parachutes anywhere to be seen. It was all most unusual. Certainly the American Government would be interested.

The explorers decided to leave the bomber as they found it and report what they had seen—through their company—to the USAF at Tripoli. They jotted down the number from the plane's twin tails—124301—and copied the lettering on the left side of the fuselage— B-24D-25-Co, AIR CORPS SER. NO. 41-24301.

Bowerman returned to Tripoli in late March, and after finishing his many survey reports, notified officials at Wheelus Air Base, in early April, of the finding of the bomber.

The story was baffling to these men, too. After a few days, noting the great distance to the reported bomber as they measured off the location on air maps, they wired their headquarters at Wiesbaden, Germany, asking for instructions about what action should be taken.

At Wiesbaden the information was equally puzzling to Air Force officers. There was no way of checking on the old B-24 in Germany, so a routine wire was transmitted to the Pentagon in Washington, requesting the past Army Air Corps' record on B-24 No. 41-24301.

After several days of Pentagon checking, the Army contacted its retired-records center in St. Louis. A few days, wires and telephone calls later, both the Army and the Air Force decided that an on-the-spot investigation was in order. The B-24 had been missing with nine American crewmen since April 4, 1943. No further information was immediately available.

2

THE *Lady Be Good* FIRST CAME into being as a purchase order to the United States by the beleaguered British government. She was to be a Consolidated Model 32 four-engined heavy bomber and was ordered under provisions of the First Defense Aid, E Program, on March 18, 1941. The airplane was part of a joint order of 629 such aircraft for use by both British and U. S. forces.

On May 12, 1941, with war clouds thickening, the United States took over the airplane order—diverting it from British use—and assigned the plane the new designation of B-24D No. 41-24301. To those who knew military specifications this designation proclaimed it to be the 24,301st aircraft ordered from the industry by the United States during the year 1941, and the fifth model of what started out as the LB-30 and was eventually redesignated as the B-24-type long-range heavy-bombardment aircraft.

She was to be manufactured in the Consolidated (now Convair Division, General Dynamics Corporation) Aircraft Corporation's California plant at San Diego. She was to have four 1,200-horsepower R-1830-C4G Twin Wasp engines of Pratt & Whitney design—air-cooled, two-row radials, with high-altitude turbosuperchargers.

Her top speed would be 316 miles an hour true air speed at 25,000 feet and she would be able to cruise at long range at 220 miles an hour at the same altitude with only 48 per cent throttle on her four engines. Eventually the plane would be armed with two-power gun turrets, one in the tail and one on the top center of her fuselage, both containing twin .50 caliber machine guns. She was also to have one .50 caliber gun on each side of her fuselage, halfway between the wing and tail, which would fire out open hatches and would be called waist guns. In her nose she was to get two more .50 caliber guns—to be fired by the navigator and the bombardier—in "flexible" mountings.

The mission of this airplane was to be heavy bombardment. To fulfill her duties in this respect, she would be able to carry 6,000 pounds of bombs 1,000 miles, drop them, and return. She could also carry a smaller bomb load farther by replacing the subtracted bomb weight with extra fuel.

In early 1942 the brand-new B-24D just coming off the assembly line in appreciable numbers was a formidable fighting machine. Along with the Boeing B-17 Flying Fortress, the B-24 Liberator was designed to, and did later help, prove the Army Air Corps' strategic airpower doctrine that had been originated a generation earlier with General "Billy" Mitchell. Until these two American long-range heavy bombers—along with their British sisters, the Lancasters, Stirlings and Halifaxes—appeared in the world's skies, the advocates of long-range strategic bombing had nothing more than blueprints and arguments for establishing their theories. The B-24, then, was a triumph over the old military theory that aircraft should be used—and could only be used profitably—as an extension of battlefield artillery or for reconnaissance. The U. S. Army Air Corps, now at war with the Axis powers, was eager to prove the B-24 in battle, and early in 1942 the first small outfits of them left the United States for Africa and the Southwest Pacific area.

A year and two days after Pearl Harbor, 41-24301 was accepted by the Air Corps' representative at San Diego, and the airplane officially "entered the Air Corps' inventory." She looked sleek, low-slung and formidable as she sat squat on the flight line with her strange pink color, her long, slim Davis wing, and her unusual tricycle landing gear. The B-24 was at that time the only heavy bomber in the world with this easy-to-handle tricycle gear. Her short nose-wheel strut brought the front of her fuselage low to the ground compared with conventional tail-wheeled bombers whose noses sat high and blind above the runways.

On February 5, 1943, two Air Corps ferrying pilots came to San Diego to pick up 41-24301. They flew her to Fort Worth, Texas, where the Consolidated Aircraft Corporation had a huge modification center. There the big bomber was specifically groomed for the type of weather and combat conditions she would experience at her destination—still secret.

By February 15th the new B-24 was properly groomed and written off as completed. She was rolled out on the Consolidated parking ramp to await the next move. As she sat among others of her type, there was nothing about 41-24301 to indicate that those who would use her as a combat weapon, and those who would later try to unravel the mystery of her lost second crew, would meet with a seemingly unending series of deaths and misadventures. From her pedigree, breeding, and physical appearance, any bomber pilot would have been proud to claim her.

A few days later she was flown to Topeka, Kansas, where she was met by the crew assigned to the bomber.

The crew was especially happy when she landed. Her color told them she was going to a desert area, where pink was good camouflage color. If she had been destined for the Southwest Pacific, she would have been painted green, and these men had already decided they preferred the Europe-Africa theater. The B-24's first assigned crew was:

2nd Lt. Samuel D. Rose, pilot
2nd Lt. Ralph O. Grace, copilot
2nd Lt. Millard B. Kesler, navigator
2nd Lt. Charles H. Midgley, bombardier
T/Sgt. William S. Nelson, engineer
Pvt. Carl L. Valentine, radio operator
Pvt. Joseph E. Maleski, asst. engineer
S/Sgt. Allyn Leavy, asst. radio operator
S/Sgt. Charles Marshall, gunner
S/Sgt. Roscoe S. Hoover, tail gunner

When the new plane began flying combat, the assistant engineer would fire one of the two waist guns, or else spell his chief. The assistant radio operator could also double as a waist gunner or serve as radio operator. A mission would require only nine of the ten-man crew, one man staying on the ground each time.

The crew's new pilot had bomber experience, though he had never been out of the States. First scheduled for the Southwest Pacific as a copilot on a B-24 back in August 1942, Lieutenant Rose's B-24 had faltered on takeoff from Hamilton Field and plunged into San Francisco Bay. The men all got out safely, but lost their aircraft, flying equipment, and personal belongings. Perhaps this accounted for Rose's wanting to be stationed in the Europe-Africa theater the next time around.

The new crew trained in an old "clunker" B-24, not considered good enough for combat, but good enough to fly around the peaceful countryside on training missions. Navigator Kesler became the unofficial documentor of the crew's life together. He kept a diary and had a good memory for details. The rest of the crew's story is his:

"The old wreck we first trained in," Kesler said, "had been named the *Lorelei* by some former crew. Lorelei was the mythical siren who lived on a rock in the Rhine River and lured boatmen to destruction with her calls. *Lorelei,* as I remember, was the fourth B-24 ever built—and you could sure tell it.

"The other crews told us *Lorelei* wouldn't fly, but we flew her without trouble on several practice missions.

"Then one day we got a flight to Patterson Field at Dayton, Ohio, to pick up a Norden bombsight. We got the bombsight okay, but when we got ready to leave, the ground crew didn't have enough 100 octane to get us back to Topeka. They said Cincinnati had plenty of fuel, so since it was only a short hop we made it.

"At Cincinnati, we refueled and started our engines to go back to Topeka. But the fuel had so much water and trash in it, that we fouled out the spark plugs before we could even taxi out for take-off. We spent a week or ten days on the ground flushing the tanks and lines and getting a new set of plugs in the four engines."

When the crew finally got back to Topeka, Kesler

said, someone suggested that when they were finally assigned their own airplane for overseas duty they should name it *Lady Be Good,* and hope the name would be a jinx-breaker.

"The name was cinched," Kesler said, "after our last local practice flight in the *Lorelei.* When we came in to land, one of the main landing-gear struts wouldn't come down, so we made a landing on the nose wheel and one main wheel—and slid sideways all the way down the runway. No one was hurt, but we had had that airplane."

This was the new crew that 41-24301 was met by on February 17, 1943. In a very short time she was no longer just a number. She had a name: *Lady Be Good.*

Kesler remembers that the crew flew her on checkout missions in February and were then given orders to take her to Morrison Field at West Palm Beach, Florida.

"On the day we were to leave—March first, nineteen forty-three—with five other pink bombers, our engineer got a case of ulcers, and we had to wait while he was hospitalized," Kesler related. "He was able to return to duty in a couple of days, so on March third we left by ourselves for Morrison hoping to catch up with the other five bombers on our flight."

But on the way down, the *Lady Be Good* ran into weather and strong headwinds, and in the growing darkness Rose landed her at Hendricks Field, Florida, for refueling. They did not get to Morrison until the

next day—just in time to see the other five pink bombers taking off for Waller Field, a lend-lease airport on
the island of Trinidad.

"From then on," Kesler says, "we flew mostly solo.
For one reason or another, we didn't get off from Morrison until March tenth. We weren't very happy either,
because we learned that instead of going to Cairo as a
final destination (which we had heard), we were only
stopping there on the way to India."

When the bomber finally reached Trinidad the other
five bombers, having had assorted troubles, were still
on the ground. The *Lady*'s crew thought it had it made
when it landed, but in his jubilation at catching up
with his group, Lieutenant Rose accidentally banged
up one of the *Lady*'s wing tips on a pile of crates while
taxiing from the runway to a hard-stand. The other
B-24s left while the *Lady* was being repaired.

However luck smiled on the *Lady*'s next two flights
to Belém and Natal, Brazil. The weather was perfect,
and they caught up with their five friends at Natal.

"For the first time all six of us left Natal together
and made the flight to Ascension Island [between South
America and Africa—a refueling stop] without incident," Kesler remembers. "This was the first time I
really checked out our radio compass ADF [Automatic
Direction Finder]. Its needle homed in perfectly on the
station at Ascension and we landed without event.
While we were on the ground there another aircraft

came in on its belly out of fuel—barely made the run-way. We began to feel lucky."

Next the bombers flew to Accra (formerly of the Gold Coast, now of Ghana). Leaving Accra, the six bombers ran into a violent sandstorm blowing off the Sahara. The *Lady*'s radio was the only one good enough, in all six planes, to receive a recall message to land, Kesler says. So the *Lady* put down at a British field at Ikeja and waited out the storm. The other five B-24s made it through the sandstorm with no further trouble—faulty radios and all—and the *Lady* again became a solo air-plane.

"Our next flight legs, to Maiduguri and Khartoum, were smooth going," Kesler remembers, "but on the last leg to Cairo we ran into trouble again. At Cairo an-other heavy sandstorm was blowing.

"We had plenty of fuel when we got there, so no one was much upset. However, the dirt-surfaced field at Heliopolis Airport—surrounded by tall buildings—was very difficult to locate through the clouds of blowing sand. We made several low-landing passes trying to line up with the field before Rose finally sneaked in for one of the prettiest landings I've ever seen. Soon after we got on the ground another B-24 bellied in out of fuel, just like the plane at Ascension. We figured that maybe the *Lady Be Good* was changing our luck for the better after all."

From Heliopolis, the crew got orders to fly the *Lady*,

not to India but to Soluch, Libya—for which they were boundlessly grateful—and to report for duty with the 376th Bomb Group. On March 23rd, they made the flight.

"Everyone at the Three Hundred and Seventy-sixth was very happy when we landed in our new ship," Kesler said. "Our plane gave the Group one more bomber than it was required to have, so the oldest plane on the field, a clunker, could be made a 'spare' ship."

Rose and his welcome crew took the *Lady* up from Soluch on March 25th for a familiarization flight around the local area, and it was then ready for the next combat mission requiring a squadron force. Meanwhile Rose went along as copilot on one mission before he was allowed to take his new plane and crew on a raid alone.

Kesler said that his crew was scheduled to make its first combat trip together in the *Lady Be Good* on April 2, 1943.

"We were going to bomb the harbor at Palermo, Sicily. But when we went out to the *Lady* after briefing, we found that our new ground crew hadn't been able to get the ship to check out properly. Looked like our luck was taking a nose dive.

"Actually it was even worse than that," Kesler went on. "When we told Operations about the *Lady*, they got in touch with Group and decided that we could fly our mission in the beat-up old spare ship that the *Lady* had made available.

"Before we ever got to the target, we began to lose
power on two engines, and a third engine cut out completely, so we dropped our bombs in the Mediterranean
and limped into the island of Malta. The Air Corps detachment there got our engines fixed late the next day,
and we took off on the fourth to go back to Soluch.

"When we got on the ground there we learned that
Bill Hatton and his crew had taken our *Lady Be Good*
on a mission to Naples. That's the last we ever saw of
the *Lady*, and we were stuck with the old spare ship
until . . . but that's another story."

The *Lady Be Good*'s jinx had just begun in earnest.
She had been assigned to Lieutenant Rose and his
crew. Next came Lieutenant Hatton and his crew. Then
the fortunes of the entire 376th Bomb Group seemed
to change for the worse—sweeping the *Lady*'s first crew
along with the tide of ill luck. And finally, many years
later, the crews of two planes searching for the *Lady*'s
lost crew in the Sahara met with disaster. Both were
using spare parts taken from the *Lady* after she was
discovered in the desert.

3

In 1941 and 1942 the United States was desperate for aircrews. From the customary 20-26 age group, the services even began to dip into the teen-age group—offering wings to high-school graduates as soon as they became 18. This lowering of standards not only pointed up a desperate quantity need but also a quality lowering through drastically shortened training programs.

The pilot-training course, then most demanding and complicated, was whittled to a mere seven and a half months; and many trainees reported to school on Saturday and began flying on Monday. Until supply and demand became reconciled, preflight schools, which measured a man's best aptitudes for training, were dispensed with. If you survived the various aircrew courses, you became an airman. If you didn't, you became a foot soldier. The incentive to graduate was powerful.

Aviation Cadet William J. Hatton, destined to become a B-24 Liberator first pilot and aircraft commander, was an "old man" when he took pilot training in 1942. Born in Jersey City, New Jersey, Hatton was 25 when he graduated from a kaleidoscope of flight phases in one year: Air Corps Primary Flying School at Avon Park, Florida, where he was taught to fly small planes by civilian instructors; Basic Flying School at Shaw Field, Sumter, South Carolina, where he first had military flight instructors; and Advanced Flying School at Spence Field, Moultrie, Georgia. When Hatton graduated from Advanced, he became a pilot and an officer, and was given his pilot's silver wings and second-lieutenant's gold bars. He was ready for combat training.

The cadet destined to be Hatton's copilot, Robert F. Toner, was even a year older. Toner was born in 1916 in Woonsocket, Rhode Island. His succession of Air Corps' flying schools ended at Columbus, Mississippi, where, in addition to finding out for certain that he was a "Yankee," he also became a second lieutenant pilot.

Two more officers were fated for Hatton's crew. Navigator Dp (a family name) Hays, then 23 and with a prematurely receding hairline that made him look older, was a native of Sedalia, Missouri. He had graduated from the Air Navigation Training School at Mather Field, Sacramento, California. At about the

same time, another old man of 26—John S. Woravka of
Cleveland, Ohio—was getting his gold bar and bombardier's wings at Albuquerque, New Mexico. Except for
Hays, the officer crew destined to fly the *Lady Be Good*
was so advanced in age by 1942 war standards that
youngsters were apt to call them "old fuds" or "Pop."

Meanwhile, 22-year-old Harold J. Ripslinger, of
Saginaw, Michigan, already a noncommissioned officer,
had graduated from the Airplane Mechanic School at
Chanute Field, Rantoul, Illinois, and was just receiv-
ing his aerial-gunner's wings at Las Vegas, Nevada.
While training, Ripslinger, who was to be Hatton's
flight engineer, met Vernon L. Moore, 21, of New
Boston, Ohio. Moore and Ripslinger graduated in the
same class, and Moore, too, was to belong to Hatton's
crew.

Three other enlisted men, in training at the time,
were also to join Hatton. Robert E. LaMotte, 22, of
Lake Linden, Michigan, was to be his radio-operator-
gunner. LaMotte had previously finished his schooling
at Scott Field, Belleville, Illinois, and was just winning
his gunner's wings at Harlingen, Texas. Guy E. Shelley,
26, of Bellaire, Ohio, graduated at Tyndall Field in
Florida; and the man who was to be Hatton's tail gunner, Samuel E. Adams, of Eureka, Illinois. Adams,
like Shelley and Moore, was to have the single crew
assignment of gunner.

In late 1942, the nine men converged, by devious
routes, at Topeka, Kansas, for training as a crew. Since

they were considerably above the average age level of those days, they must have been pleased with the nine sets of individual orders that had brought them together —by the purest chance of alphabetical listings-by-specialty.

And the seven men who were to rely on the two pilots to fly them safely must have been relieved at getting mature officers. At the same time, the "old" pilots probably welcomed a heavy-bomber assignment: There was something quite grown-up and reassuring about a B-24. Let the "hot" youngsters fly the dazzling new Warhawk, Lightning and Airacobra fighters, and leave the big ones to the men.

A bombardier, of course, was going to fly in bombers —period. But the B-24 was no medium bomber; it was one of the two queens of all bombers, and ample reason for pride on the part of John Woravka. Besides, the heavy bombers could take more punishment, and flew at higher altitudes—farther away from antiaircraft flak.

As for Dp Hays, he knew that navigators were scorned and thought useless in other than combat outfits where there was enough glory to go around—even to navigators.

For the gunners, the engineer and radio operator, it was extremely satisfying to be going into battle in the heavyweight class with caliber .50 machine guns—and to be getting 50 per cent extra pay for hazardous "duties involving frequent aerial flight"; a bonus that gravel-grinding ground crews could never get. And none of the crew felt that they would have to "back through the pay line at the end of the month," embarrassed at not having really earned their money.

It was cold in Topeka as 1943 began. Training in B-24s too old or too nonstandard to fight began immediately. Many mornings, the men had to clear icicles from the trailing edges of the wings and tail before they could fly.

Training consisted of teaching each man his precise job as it related to a B-24, and then, under the pilot's command, learning to operate together as a skilled team.

Each of them was awed, at first, by the roaring power of the combined 4,800 horses in their four Pratt & Whitney engines, and by the then-enormous size of the bomber (over 60,000 pounds loaded) and its "hot" 110-mile-per-hour landing speed.

Training went well despite initial timidity and uncertainty, and one day the men were told that in February a brand-new B-24D would be flown to Topeka and would become their personal weapon. Crew and airplane assignments were posted on the operations-room bulletin board, and under Hatton's name was B-24D No. 42-40081. Somewhere down the line the bomber was getting final combat modifications. Then the men would have themselves a bomber—and an overseas' assignment.

When 42-40081 smacked onto the runway with twin

puffs of blue smoke and scrunchings of rubber tires in early February, her new crew was on hand to welcome her. Each man sweated out the B-24 as it was taxied from the runway to the parking ramp. Nine pairs of eyes watched every move. Suppose the ferry pilots goofed up their new plane before they got it parked? But the big ship was skillfully guided into the parking slot without incident, the four engines were cut, and the new crew swarmed over it.

For the next two weeks, Hatton and his men flew extensive checkout missions, and every inch of the big plane's complex mechanism was checked meticulously.

Late in the month the B-24D and her crew were ready to go. Administrative orders temporarily assigned six B-24Ds to the Caribbean Wing of the Air Transport Command so the men could fly their badly needed bombers to a combat front. The 3-year tide of war, so humiliatingly in favor of the enemy until recently, *must* be reversed.

Pilots were Lieutenants Goehry, Bennett, Fallon, Hatton, McAtee and Foster. The six crews left together for Morrison and stayed there only long enough to get new orders assigning them overseas.

Operations Order No. 93, dated February 28, 1943, ordered the six crews slated for temporary duty with Caribbean Air Command to: ". . . proceed in aircraft as indicated from Morrison Field, West Palm Beach, Florida, to Cairo, Egypt, reporting upon arrival thereat to the Commanding Officer, Ninth Air Force, for duty and assignment."

As soon as the weather down the South Atlantic ferrying route was good, the six bombers headed out over the beautiful West Indian island chain. The crews were stirred by the novelty of this new environment of throbbing engines moving toward strange, far-off places.

Cairo? There had been articles in the newspapers and scenes on the newsreels about the Army Air Forces operating with the British across the Northeast African Desert. There had been names like Mersa Matrûh, El Alamein, Tobruk and Sidi Barrâni. Maybe the Allies were starting a big buildup over there, now that Rommel was on the run. Each new airman felt a glow of beginning achievement—and a deep responsibility—as they roared over the quiet necklace of islands.

One of the first direct U. S. military efforts to help its ailing Allies on the world-wide fronts was the Halverson Detachment (named for the Air Corps officer charged with conducting it). This was a 1942 top-secret program to provide assistance to the beleaguered British Eighth Army in the Near East. British General Archibald P. Wavell, with his back to the wall of Alexandria and Cairo, had to somehow keep Rommel's German Afrika Korps away from the Suez Canal—one of the most vital Allied life lines; indeed the key to the defense of the entire Middle East.

Part of the Halverson Project consisted of flying a group of then-untried B-24 Liberator bombers to Fayid, Egypt, to provide a heavy-bomber force for Wavell. There were two B-24 groups organized from the Halverson Detachment and put at Wavell's disposal in a very short time; the 98th and the 376th. The 98th was commanded by Colonel John R. "Killer" Kane, and the 376th by 25-year-old Colonel Keith K. Compton.

When, in October 1942, British General Bernard L. Montgomery—field commander for General Harold R. Alexander, who had replaced Wavell in supreme command of the Middle East forces—led his Eighth Army in a complete breakup of Rommel's forces at El Alamein, B-24s of the Halverson Detachment were a part of this first great Anglo-American victory. Until then there had been only one large-scale Allied victory— that of the Russians at Stalingrad. Prior to El Alamein, those flying the B-24s had been forced to retreat ahead of Rommel all the way to Palestine in order to keep their bombers safe from the shorter-ranged Messerschmitts and Junkers of the Luftwaffe. So the victory at Alamein was sweet, not only to the British, but also to the Americans who had helped pound Rommel's behind-the-lines forces with their long-range strategic bombers—untried weapons which had been suspect and discredited up to 1942.

Kane's and Compton's men moved their bases forward as the British again wound westward along the coast of Egypt and then Libya.

When, in January 1943, General Montgomery had pummeled Rommel's crack Korps back through Tripoli, it became safe to move the heavy bombers to liberated Benghazi. The closest German bombers which could catch them on the ground were in Sicily, Italy and Crete. Luftwaffe bombers were not geared for long range with a heavy bomb load, and their pilots shied away from round trips of that distance when only a token load could be carried.

By March, the Ninth "Desert" Air Force was in business in Benghazi. In forward areas closer to the front, at that time in Tunisia, the Ninth operated B-25 Mitchell medium bombers and P-40 Warhawk fighters alongside the British Royal Air Force, and the Aussies, and South Africans they were helping. The Ninth Bomber Command was composed of "Killer" Kane's 98th Group and Keith Compton's 376th, which had come to be known as the "Liberandos." Its mission was to strike the enemy where it hurt most: his otherwise safe supply ports, railroad-marshaling yards, factories producing war material, bridges, and airfields far behind the lines. The first targets would be in Sicily and Italy; later the bombers would range into the Balkan countries.

Almost a year before, the B-24s had served notice on Hitler and Mussolini (just as Lieutenant Colonel

Jimmy Doolittle had served notice on Hirohito with his carrier-launched B-25 strike on Tokyo). A paltry force of 13 B-24s operating from Fayid, Egypt, before the humiliating retreat to Palestine, had struck the first American blow on June 12, 1942 at what was listed as the number-one Axis target in Europe, the Ploesti oilfields in Romania. The planes struck from high altitude, did little damage, and their losses were proportionately small, but (just as in Japan) the raid caused the defenders to deploy large fighter and antiaircraft forces to protect the area. The fighters and guns idled around Ploesti for 15 months when they were urgently needed elsewhere. The Luftwaffe was taking no chances that the American Air Force did not have sufficient strength to return with its heavies. The fact was that the strength was more urgently needed for a while for other more immediate targets on the route to Southern Europe.

So in March 1943, operating from several airfields in the Benghazi area, the Ninth, under Brigadier General Uzal Ent, had several immediate targets. Operating with other B-24s and B-17 Flying Fortresses flying out of Algeria, Ent's B-24s were to pulverize deep strategic targets in Sicily and Italy—for a very good reason. The Allies were confident of an early victory over Rommel's almost bottled-up forces in Tunisia, and an early invasion of Sicily was planned. (On May 12, 1943, German Colonel General Von Arnim and Italian Field Marshal Messe surrendered 248,000 men near historic Zama, on the Cape Bon, or Ras Addar, peninsula; echoing the historic defeat of Hannibal of Carthage there hundreds of years earlier at the hands of the Romans.)

The Sicilian invasion was the first large-scale triphibious joint Allied invasion attempt of the war against a defended territory. It could succeed only if the enemy's air strength was knocked down to an effective minimum and his seaborne means of resupply, as well as the supplies themselves, were either destroyed or their movement prevented. This was the job of the heavy strategic bombers, and this is what they set about doing in earnest in early 1943.

Keith Compton's Group was first settled at the little village of Soluch, 25 miles southeast of Benghazi. The Soluch airfield was a barren flat scar, bulldozed level through hard desert sand. There was not a sign of pavement, either for runways, taxiways, hard-stands, automobiles—or anything.

Most important to everyone's well-being was the flock of heavy-bellied tricycle-geared bombers. There were tarpaulins to cover the engines at night and during the frequent sandstorms, and everyone from aircrew to mechanic and plain ground-pounder treated the B-24s with respect and favoritism. When the bombers' engines were run up for test or for actual take-off on a mission, a veritable hurricane of fine, gritty red-brown sand blew for hundreds of yards behind and up. Aircraft and men alike lived in its constant bite and sting— and neither was designed to take it. The bombers had

troubles with engines, instruments, oxygen and hydraulic lines, engine oil filters. The men merely had diar-
rhea, dysentery, yellow jaundice and sore eyes from
sand, dust-borne grit and assorted bacteria. And what
happened to human respiratory systems has not yet
been medically chronicled.

Living in sand, the bombers had tarpaulins—the men
had tents. The bombers ate gasoline and oil with sand
mixed in, and the men ate sand-filled food and drank
gritty water. The Libyan *ghibli* winds blew sand and
heat from the Sahara in the south and blew tarpaulins
off B-24 engines while blowing down headquarters
tents, living quarters and mess tents. Water was as
scarce and essential as 100-octane gasoline. It was no
easy way to fight a war, but the Germans had done it,
and the Italians, and the British—and if they could survive, so could Americans.

The big wooden crates the bombs came in were immediately "requisitioned" to make furniture for tents
and slabbing for shoring up wind-whipped tent bot-
toms. After so long a time, it was possible for an old
crew to have the luxury of a partial wooden tent floor.
Men bathed and shaved out of their helmets—when
there was water. For recreation—an occasional outdoor
movie on a screen made of bomb-crate wood, while ap-
plying a vile-smelling mosquito lotion and slapping off
bugs that weren't bothered by it at all. If you had seen
the movie months before in the States, you could listen
to Mildred Gillars, sweet-voiced "Axis Sally," telling

"all you American boys out there" about how your girl friends and wives were running around with draft dodgers back home. Sally's sirupy voice would ask, "Don't you wish you were back home now, with your best girl?" That line was always good for laughs. The roared answer: "Hell no, babe! I've found a home in this blasted desert!"

Combat-mission briefings were conducted at the outdoor theater, using the "movie screen" as a blackboard for operations and intelligence maps. Almost everything was out in the open, including the one-holer latrines made of fuel drums stuck two-thirds of the way down in the sand with both ends cut out. Primitive bomb-crate-wood tops were made into seats and covers to keep out germ-carrying flies. As soon as a latrine hole was filled, the drum was moved over a few feet, and the top of the old hole covered with sand. During all daylight hours the men were watched in all their actions by curious, impassive Arabs who moved in and out of the tents, trading, looking, listening. Some said there were German spies among them. Maybe so, but how could you tell? And how could you keep the Arabs off the so-called airport? Build a fence? Use half your men as guards while the other half worked on, and flew, the bombers?

It was from bleak Soluch that devastating bomb raids were launched in early 1943 against a comfortable enemy, well housed, well clothed and well fed, living in the civilized areas of Sicily and Italy. It was galling to

the men of the 376th to think how much better off the
enemy probably was, but they were determined that
this would not last forever—not as long as the B-24s
would fly.

Into the hectic sand bowl of East Libya, from the replacement depot in Cairo, came trickles of new aircrews and new B-24s to replace those shot down, or to
augment the too-small maintenance-ridden forces of
heavy bombers.

In late March Hatton and Toner landed their B-24D
at Heliopolis Airport in Cairo, bringing a needed
brand-new bomber for the Ninth Bomber Command,
and a welcome relief crew.

Hatton and his men were assigned to the 376th Bomb
Group, 514th Squadron; the other five who had flown
over with them went to other squadrons of the two
Groups at Soluch-Benghazi. With just enough time to
sign in and out, Hatton's crew fired up and flew to
Soluch. It was March 27, 1943. A sad date for the crew.
The 514th squadron had more crews than it had B-24s,
so 42-40081 went to an older team, and Hatton's became
a spare crew without a plane.

The nine men took a couple of days to get settled
down in the squadron area—drawing supplies, bedding,
cots, mosquito netting, getting assigned to tents, finding
the makeshift mess hall, etc. Then Hatton and Toner
were taken on an orientation flight, and Hatton was
told that he would soon draw one mission as a copilot.

After that single mission he would be considered checked out again as a first pilot—and ready for a combat mission with his crew. Others of Hatton's crew would go along as passenger-observers in other B-24s on the same flight. Then the nine men would be ready to tackle the Luftwaffe and Axis antiaircraft fire.

While waiting for their first familiarization mission, and sweating out mail call for first letters from home, Hatton and Hays were loafing around in the sand one morning when Captain Martin R. Walsh, a squadron old-timer, walked up.

"How would you two fellows like to take a little trip to Cairo and back with me?" Walsh asked.

"Cairo! You bet!" both men chorused. "They didn't even give us time to fly *over* the town on the way in."

Walsh had drawn an administrative flight back to the lush Near East metropolis, and had room for a copilot and a navigator.

"They weren't doing anything else," Walsh recalled years later, "and they looked sort of lost—as newcomers will. I thought they'd like to take a break.

"We were supposed to come right back to Soluch," he continued, "but when we were taking off from Heliopolis—what do you know? One of our engines cut out! We got her stopped okay, but the engine had to be changed, and that took another day, unfortunately.

"As long as we had to be in town anyway, the three of us went out to the Pyramids at Giza and had our pictures taken sitting in front of the Sphinx on some camels."

When the three men got back to Soluch, Hatton got his assignment as copilot to First Lieutenant R. F. Hurd to fly a Palermo, Sicily, harbor raid on April 2nd. The mission was an abort because of weather, but short as the 376th was of trained crews, it was considered sufficient as a check-out for the Hatton crew. After all, the men had flown a B-24 from the States without any trouble, and Hatton was the same age as the group commander, and Toner was a year older.

On April 4th, Hatton and his crew got a break. Lieutenant Rose's B-24, which he had named *Lady Be Good,* was out in the sand ready to fly, and Rose and his crew were in Malta with engine trouble on another B-24. The squadron needed a replacement crew, and Hatton's was it. They were to go on a 25-plane high-altitude raid on Naples. It was a well-planned raid: The B-24s were to go into Naples at 25,000 feet in broad daylight and hit the target just at sunset. They could then break formation and come home singly under cover of darkness. In the absence of escorting fighters, which then had insufficient range for long flights, darkness was a welcome condition for a bomber dodging Luftwaffe night fighters.

The raid fouled up badly in the second section of the formation—with which Hatton was flying. The first section tore up the target, and every plane in it got shot up. But the second section took off with too much blowing sand in its air scoops, and most of the planes lost the use of one or more engines. None of them made it to the target.

At the stand-up breakfast the next morning, eaten off a high bench out in the open, word passed along that the new fellow, Hatton, and Lieutenant Iovine—in B-24 No. 31—hadn't made it back from Naples. But while they still were eating, a call from Group said that Iovine had got into Malta okay on the way home. Where the devil was Hatton?

Someone said he heard that Hatton had broken radio silence and called for an emergency bearing from the RDF Station. Worley and Swarner said that Hatton had been with them clear up to Sorrento before they turned back after sunset. Well. That's what it was, then. The Hatton crew's first mission; they must have gotten lost coming back in the dark and run out of fuel. Ditched in the sea, probably. One pilot said he heard that Operations was sending out an air search. The search boys would find them all right—floating around in their rafts.

Contacted after the discovery of the *Lady* in the desert, Ralph Grace, original copilot of the bomber crew which flew the ship to Libya, recalled that he had heard a B-24 passing directly over Soluch airfield, headed southeast, some time before midnight and after all planes that were to return from the Naples raid were on the ground. He commented on it at the time, but the remark was lost in other speculation and not seriously considered for after all, it could have been a plane from another group going over. Or perhaps he had mistaken the sound of a night fighter for that of a heavy bomber. It could have been one of a number of possibilities. Who knew? Only one thing was certain at that time: a check disclosed that Hatton had called for an *inbound* bearing *after* Grace heard what he thought was the *Lady* passing over the airfield on a heading which would take it into the desert.

Several days later, with still no news, one of the pilots suggested that a German night fighter had picked up Hatton's radio transmission for a bearing, homed in on the B-24, and shot it down over the water. That seemed about as likely as anything.

By then the 376th had already moved to Berca No. 2.

4

For THE FIRST FEW WEEKS after the discovery of the B-24 in the Libyan desert it seemed that the tangled mystery of the *Lady Be Good* and her nine men would never be unraveled. Every new skein of fact, carefully culled from the 16-year-old Army Air Corps' records, seemed to lead only to another frustrating snarl.

Old operations orders, mission reports, old "secret" messages, Intelligence debriefings of the 24 crews which returned from the April 4, 1943 Naples raid—all failed to spotlight any clarity, so far as Hatton and his crew were concerned. Name after name of participating crewmen was traced to its owner, only to result in clouded recollections, memories that proved imperfect, or the stark statistics: "Killed [Died, or Missing] In

Action." Of the first dozen or so former members of the 376th Bomb Group who were found, none were personally acquainted with any member of Hatton's crew, and few knew more of the affair than they had read in the newspapers.

First Lieutenant Paul J. Fallon was the first to remember enough detail to make any evaluation of recorded facts rewarding.

Intelligence records showed that Fallon had been a first pilot in Section A, the leading section of the Naples raiders, on April 4, 1943. While Hatton's *Lady Be Good* was in Section B during the raid, it was nevertheless noted that Fallon and Hatton and their two crews appeared together on several military orders in early 1943. There was every chance that Fallon would have known Hatton personally.

Contacted by telephone in Dayton, Ohio, where he was stationed then as a major at Wright-Patterson Air Force Base, Fallon's detailed description, in July 1959, of his actions 16 years earlier tallied almost precisely with reports of the raid—and almost unbelievably with his own Intelligence report given at 11 p.m. April 4, 1943. His recollections helped bridge previously unrelated events and led to new inquiries with new people. Together, they helped light the labyrinth of dozens of previously undigestible mission reports by individual crews.

"Yes, I knew Bill Hatton well," Fallon recalled. "We

went through B-24 operational training together. Bill got married just before we went overseas, and a bunch of us attended his wedding.

"We had all checked out as crews on the B-24s at Topeka, and then ferried our planes to Morrison Field at West Palm Beach, Florida, and on over to Egypt. At Heliopolis Airport, Cairo, Hatton and I were assigned to the Three Hundred and Seventy-sixth Bomb Group on the same orders, and we left in a few days for our first combat assignment at Soluch, Libya."

Fallon vividly remembered the April 4th Naples raid. "Hatton, you see, was the first friend of mine who was lost in action. You don't forget something like that.

"He was in the second section when we took off from Soluch for Naples. I wouldn't likely forget the details, because it was a rough raid and was only my third mission. When we got to the Group we were assigned to different squadrons, and it was hard to keep in touch. I saw Bill after my first mission, and he hadn't been on one yet.

"The afternoon of the Naples raid, we took off from Soluch in a sandstorm, and Section A, which I was flying in, formed up and headed out on a long climb toward Italy. Section B took off next and followed us."

Fallon said that his section was slated to hit the Naples harbor with its bombs just about nightfall.

"We went over the target in formation," Fallon said, "and dropped our bombs. I remember seeing the bombs fall on the target, and later this was verified by photo-reconnaissance planes. But over the target there was one awful lot of flak from the antiaircraft guns. My plane was hit several times and some of my control cables were shot away. It was kind of hard to fly the old bird like that, but none of my crew was hurt. After the target, we flew formation for a little way south until it got dark, then we broke up and went home alone.

"I went down to low altitude along the Italian west coast in order to avoid night fighters as much as possible, flew by the island of Stromboli, then Sicily, and finally took up a dead-reckoning course for Soluch. I remember how careful we were to keep on course, because when we got back all we had at Soluch was a very low-power light beacon and a low-power homer-radio beacon to help us in.

"We got there all right and found the beacons and landed," Fallon remembered. "It was very dark, and if we had not been on course, or had not noticed the seacoast when we crossed it, we could easily have gone right on by and out over the desert without ever realizing it. The coast, of course, was blacked out and very difficult to see—especially from anything but a low altitude. And the desert looked gray, like the sea at night, so the only way you'd know the difference was if you noticed the slight, light line of breakers on the beach as you flew over. I don't want to make it sound harder than it was, because if you were exactly on course you couldn't miss. But if you were too high, and didn't turn on your radio compass while you were in range, you could get in trouble very easily."

About Hatton's last flight, Fallon only remembered that his friend had not returned that night, and that all the men he knew were thoroughly puzzled about what might have happened.

"It was anyone's guess," Fallon said. "The war moved along pretty fast just then, and we never did learn what happened to Bill. As a matter of fact, we moved to another base in just a few days, and flew more missions, moved again and so on. It was hard to keep track of things under those conditions."

But Fallon also offered other names of 376th Bomb Group pilots still living who should be able to add further clarification. These men were eventually found, and gradually the World War II records began to come into focus.

Wartime operational records had not been designed to answer individual questions in detail. Their purpose was to provide a quick wide-angle view of each day's combat with the enemy. They were written for commanders—to give them an instant daily run-down of the previous day's actions and of the combat resources (men, planes, bombs, ammunition, fuel) available for the current day's air battles. Tracking individual actions through these reports often depended on luck rather than upon knowledge of what to look for.

While the desert search for the *Lady Be Good*'s crewmen continued to turn up only continuing confusion, the search for facts in the United States was more promising. By September, 1959, thanks to the many who verified and "translated" piecemeal bits of knowledge and shreds of facts, it was possible to begin to reconstruct the Naples raid.

On April 4, 1943, the American Army Air Forces in Algeria and Libya had drawn a deadly bead on Naples—its defenses, its airfields and its important harbor. Naples was at that time a central port for sea-borne and air-borne movements to resupply the fast-crumbling Axis forces in Tunisia. The Axis was even more aware of the port's importance. An enormous and deadly combination of defense forces was committed to protect the city.

Against a conglomerate of targets, three raids by B-17 Flying Fortresses were scheduled on April 4 from Algerian bases, and one by B-24 from Soluch. One hundred and six B-17s took off from Algeria to attack Capodichino and the harbor and marshalling yards at Naples, dropping a gigantic total of 420,320 pounds of bombs.

A typical section of the complete then-secret operational report of the Soluch Group, after completion of the raid, reads:

Twenty five B-24Ds of the 376th Bomb Group took off from Soluch at 1130 GMT to bomb NAPLES harbor. 72 x 500 lb. American .10 nose .025 tail fuse bombs dropped on target at 1735-45 GMT from 23,500 to 25,-000 feet. Hits observed at pin points M-40; MN 46, 47; K-41; J-40; M-47; Map N/2(2). Target clear with ground haze. Antiaircraft fire heavy and intense for range and altitude. A/C 33 Lt. Critchfield No. 4 engine shot out, No. 1 engine hit. A/C 34 Capt. Hoover flesh wound on neck. A/C 45 Lt. Lear holed over Crotone. One ship reports seeing about 12 unidentified fighters coming up after formation. Three hit by own A/A, remainder turned away. No attack. Large M/V seen leaving Gulf of Naples heading SSE. Dust at landing field [on takeoff] caused substantial engine trouble resulting in numerous turn-backs. A/C 95 Lt. Gluck and A/C 37 Lt. Flavelle reported at Malta. A/C 64 Lt. Hatton and A/C 31 Lt. Iovine unaccounted for

The Axis supply center at Naples, as well as its defenses, had known a gruelling day, and the American bombers returned with minute losses compared to the opposition and the damage they had inflicted. The following morning, when it was discovered that Lieutenant Iovine had returned safely as far as the British island of Malta, the score of losses totaled only one B-24 —Hatton's *Lady Be Good,* with the large white numerals 64 painted on each side of the nose.

Only one cognate fact was conclusive from the debriefings of the 24 crews that returned. Section B in which the *Lady* was flying had never reached Naples. All the B-24s in the Section had turned about for one reason or another, and flown back to Soluch without reaching the primary target. Thirteen B-24s had made up Section B, and with the first light of a desert dawn at Soluch, Intelligence officers had interviewed 11 crews of the Section. A twelfth crew had been queried by the British at Malta.

In the debriefing of one pilot—the last to land at Soluch that night—lay the one positive clue to the *Lady*'s part in the mission. It was duly entered in an Intelligence report, but the war moved on and the clue went unnoticed. It was not noticed, in fact, for more than 16 years—even though exhaustive boards of inquiry met often and worked diligently. The ever-growing voluminous records, like the war, were borne back and forth across countries and oceans. Boards of inquiry, meeting overseas, had no access to the growing morass of folders, boxes and bales of records sent to the United States for segregation and filing. The boards, then, acted upon whatever accumulated evidence was relative. Based upon this growing fact pile in this one file, the boards reached a decision—one isolated decision among the thousands required of them.

The first action toward finding the *Lady Be Good* and her crew was not a board action, but an operational one.

On the morning of April 5, 1943, unaware of that one vital jigsaw piece of information which would have led them in the right direction, Army Air Corps rescue-and-search personnel made an extensive aerial reconnaissance from the airport at Soluch, shadowing the general coastal area next to the Gulf of Sirte, around the Mediterranean Sea, and back in the direction of a crow's flight from Soluch to Naples. Conjecture about the *Lady*'s probable point of landing stemmed from a report made by the Radio Direction Finder Station at Benina (the master airport in the Benghazi system of landing fields). The RDF Station log read that Lieutenant Hatton had requested an *inbound* emergency bearing at 12:12 A.M. April 5th. The station said it reported to Hatton that he was on a 330-degree magnetic bearing from Benina. Hatton was silent after that, station personnel said. But with the inbound bearing in the precise direction (the north-northwest) from which the *Lady Be Good* should have been flying, the searchers assumed that Hatton and his crew had ditched the *Lady* in the Mediterranean en route back to Soluch.

Rescuers reported having conducted an all-out search. They said they found no life rafts or any other evidence of a water crash such as oil slicks or floating debris. There was no trace of plane No. 64 along the coast, either. The search was abandoned.

Next of kin were notified that the nine-man crew and its airplane were missing in action. Relatives could still hope that their husbands, sons or brothers might have been shot down and captured by the enemy, but not yet reported through the International Red Cross.

World War II catapulted on. By April 5, 1944—a year later—the invasion of Normandy was only two months away. The Allies had taken Tunisia, Pantelleria in Sicily, and much of Italy—including all the area around Naples and south in which the *Lady Be Good* might have crashed inland or near the shore. On April 5, 1944, a board of officers was convened, under provisions of the Missing Persons Act, to re-examine all known evidence surrounding this disappearance. With the sparse facts available, plus all reports of known crashed American aircraft (but without the key pilot report which still was in the traveling files of the 376th Bomb Group), the board changed the status of Lieutenant Hatton's crew to "Missing in action and presumed dead." Next of kin were notified. Until the "presumed dead" was added, it had been easier to hope. Now the hope faded. As of April 5, 1944, these nine men became legally dead.

When the war was over, an exhaustive inquiry about Hatton and his men left little doubt (but still a little) in the minds of the crewmen's relatives. The inquiry was made by a formal board, meeting in the former Axis co-capital of Rome on April 10, 1946. Officers of the board stated that they had considered captured German and Italian records, reviewed searches conducted over Italian coast lines (including many interviews with Italian fishermen), scanned records of American aircraft crashes on the lower Italian peninsula, and gone over interviews with prisoners of war who might conceivably have furnished clues. Their verdict was that, in the light of all existing facts, Lieutenant Hatton's crew had presumably been killed in action.

Two years later a final seven-officer board of inquiry, representing the U. S. Army's American Graves Registration Service, met in Rome on June 15, 1948, to once again look at the record. After more than three years, the board said, it could realistically be assumed that every possible pertinent fact about Lieutenant Hatton and his crew would have been available. This board reviewed the entire case—including the results of all previous boards' findings and the original air search—and examined every record of American casualties amassed since the war.

It determined that every possible effort had been made to find the nine missing crewmen, and that they were presumed to have crashed in the Mediterranean without leaving a trace. The board's report was endorsed as valid all the way through the War Department in Washington; relatives were notified of the final action.

But this board, like all its predecessors, lacked one key document: The Intelligence debriefing of the last pilot known to land at Soluch after the April 4, 1943, raid on Naples harbor.

This one unnoticed, unlocking report was made by First Lieutenant Luther A. Worley. In it was a partial sentence which pointed directly to where the *Lady Be Good* had gone down: ". . . think the leader was number sixty-four." It was this single remark, among the thousands made following the four April 4th raids on Naples, which dovetailed the scattered pieces of the *Lady*'s story.

In July, 1959, the sentence was unearthed by accident when every known report about the raid was being painstakingly sifted. The search for any reference to "Lieutenant Hatton," "No. 64,"—or any possible path through the maze—produced only this one statement having even slight bearing on Hatton's plane. It was literally the only reference to the plane by any of the 24 crews of the 376th Bomb Group who returned safely from the Naples mission. Based on Lieutenant Worley's broken sentence, and the time at which it was made, it was possible for Department of Defense officers to reconstruct the mission in detail—even though this reconstruction was, of necessity, largely guesswork.

A Department of Defense "fact sheet" on the *Lady*'s mission was published on July 27, 1959, detailing— from the Group's individual mission reports—the exact flights of twelve of the thirteen B-24s which flew in Section B. After outlining the reasons for which nine of the B-24s of the Section had turned back before reaching the target, the fact sheet, relying heavily upon Lieutenant Worley's partial sentence, but without clearer proof, reported:

"Lt. Hatton apparently assumed lead of the remaining four airplanes at 7:25 P.M., according to the mission report by Lt. L. A. Worley who was flying number-two position [right wing] by this time. The two other air-craft still in formation were flown by Lt. W. C. Swarner and Lt. E. L. Gluck."

On that night of April 4th, Swarner landed safely back at Soluch at 10:45. If he mentioned having been one of the last three planes flying behind Hatton, his Intelligence debriefer did not record the fact on his mission report. Twenty-six days later Swarner was killed in action.

Since fuel shortage had forced Gluck to land at Malta, his mission report—given to British Intelligence there—would have taken some time to reach the 376th through military channels.

Lieutenant Worley also landed back at Soluch the night of April 4th. His was the last of the twenty-four B-24s ticked in after the day's action. Exactly three months later Worley was reported missing in action. A year later this was changed to "Missing in action and presumed dead"—the same pattern taken with Hatton's crew. Worley's status remains unchanged today.

On that important morning of April 5th, it seems probable that many in the 376th Bomb Group had only half of the facts necessary to conclude where the *Lady Be Good* might have gone down. Only two were necessary. The first was Lieutenant Worley's statement that about 7:50 P.M. April 4th he thought he was following No. 64. The second was the *time*—12:12 A.M.—that Benina RDF Station logged a supposed emergency request for an *inbound* bearing for the *Lady*. When put together, these two facts bore out Lieutenant Grace's report that he had heard a B-24 over Soluch airfield, heading southeast, before midnight.

Whether any member of the 376th Bomb Group learned of both the necessary facts is impossible to determine. But if anyone had possessed both bits of information, and had realized that Hatton's aircraft had been in formation with Worley, Swarner and Gluck until after dark in the vicinity of Naples, had noticed that Worley—the last man to the ground—had landed at 11:10 P.M. at Soluch, and had then noticed that Hatton's request for an *inbound* bearing came one hour and two minutes *after* the last airplane in his formation had landed, there would have at least been doubt that the Hatton plane was down in the Mediterranean. It would have been thought wise to search the inbound course for some distance beyond Soluch—although it seems doubtful that any search of more than 100 miles past the airfield and into the desert would have been recommended. But at least this search would have been in the right direction; and some pilot just might have flown far enough into the desert to find the crewmen.

The circumstances under which the necessary clues to the *Lady Be Good*'s disappearance became known to various people hardly justified such clear, efficient evaluation as would have been required to find Hatton's crew.

The three other planes of the four-plane formation

were debriefed immediately after landing by parched, sand-gritted, tired Intelligence officers (both American and British) in crude blacked-out tents or bombed-out pieces of buildings. The men worked steadily through the night debriefing exhausted aircrews. Then they had to fit together urgent action-and-result reports for higher headquarters, so that strategy could be mapped early the next morning for the April 6th raid. Without detailed planning the B-24s could count on maximum losses from enemy actions and minimum damage to enemy targets. This planning had top priority. Almost as soon as the debriefings and reports were accomplished, Intelligence was neck-deep in collecting information for its own part in briefing aircrews for the April 6th raid. If it was told about the 12:12 A.M. emergency-bearing request from No. 64 this information was never recorded. Even so, it is doubtful, with the exhaustion that prevailed, whether the fact would have had any immediate significance for them. Their job was to keep abreast of enemy activities and the results of American actions against those enemies. They were not pilots or navigators, and this information related to special aircrew problems; to time and distance, courses and altitudes, and winds aloft.

At the same time, Operations officers—all of whom were pilots—who had received the information from Benina about Hatton's emergency call, had also worked late into the night. Some had flown the mission to Naples and landed back at Soluch with shot-up B-24s and scared crews. They too were spent. They too were evaluating the results of the day's raid while planning operational aspects of the April 6th mission. If Operations had taken time to read all the Intelligence debriefings in detail, they would probably never have gotten the April 6th mission off the ground. They depended upon Intelligence to tell them what they should know.

Intelligence, unskilled in problems of flight itself, depended upon Operations to ask the right questions concerning its own areas of responsibility. And both Operations and Intelligence were dog-tired.

Meanwhile, command and administrative people—a conceivable bridge between Operations and Intelligence—were also working through the night. They had too many urgent matters to consider, accomplish, head off or nullify: repairs of shot-up aircraft, changing of ailing B-24 engines, moving to Berca airfield, supplies, blood plasma, parachute packing, ammunition, machine-gun repairing, coding and sending urgent reports, decoding incoming secret orders, arranging for replacement crews and planes, Red Cross supplies, quinine for aircrews, atabrine for ground crews. They too had their hands full. Operations and Intelligence simply had to carry through on their own.

Thus two contradictory facts were not joined for many years—at least they were not related properly to spell out a correct conclusion. If anyone did notice the contradiction at the time, that extra hour that Benina RDF reported the *Lady Be Good* had taken to get *in-*

bound to Soluch was probably dismissed as due to engine failure or the plane's having been shot down. Everyone in the 376th Bomb Group clung to the idea that No. 64 had gone down in the Mediterranean. No one really had time for any detailed analysis. Before such an investigation could even have been started, there were more missions, more missing planes, more mysteries, more dead, more wounded and more men injured in landing accidents.

Unusual problems could demand no priority. They would be solved after the war ended . . . if at all.

5

THE STORY OF THE Libyan Desert mystery bomber was first given to American news-wire services by Headquarters, United States Air Forces in Europe at Wiesbaden.

An Associated Press report datelined Wiesbaden, June 4, 1959, read:

> A special team of investigators has been charged with looking into the wartime crash of an American Liberator bomber in the Libyan Desert 16 years ago, the U. S. Air Force reported today.
>
> It said the discovery of the big bomber in the trackless wastes has presented one of the greatest air mysteries of modern times.
>
> The World War II craft was discovered recently lying fully visible on hard-packed sand 380 miles south of

Benghazi by a geological research team of a prospecting oil company.

The geologists' reports have been verified in a nine-hour reconnaissance flight of an Air Force rescue plane.

According to today's announcement, the big question is whether any of the Liberator's crew survived the belly landing. If so, where are they; if not where are the remains?

The day after this story broke, the Associated Press Bureau in Washington dug into the report with Department of Defense press officers. In a release from Washington the same day, the AP said:

The Pentagon made public tonight the names of crewmen last known to be aboard a B-24 bomber which made an amazing landing in the Libyan Desert 16 years ago.

The plane, almost undamaged and wholly untouched, was reported found recently by a team of exploring geologists. There was no trace of the crew.

An Air Force spokesman in Wiesbaden, Germany, speculated that the crew had bailed out after a bombing raid on Naples in 1943, and that the plane landed on its own.

In making public the names of crewmen, the Pentagon said it had not yet determined how they are listed in casualty records. That information is contained in stored files.

The Army said the mystery wreckage was that of a bomber which left Soluch, Libya, on April 4, 1943, for

a high-altitude bombing mission against Naples, Italy.
The intended course toward the target was not known
nor was it known whether the plane actually reached
its target, the Army said.

The wreckage was located 380 miles south of Benghazi.

The Army is investigating the case because during
World War II the Air Force, then called the Air Corps,
was part of the Army.

A two-man team from the Mortuary Service Headquarters at Frankfurt, Germany, flew to the area on
May 11. An aerial survey has been made and a ground
search of the area was planned, Army Headquarters
here said.

In making public the names of the crewmen, the
Army emphasized that the addresses and next of kin
are taken from 1943 files, presumably outdated in many
cases.

The story then listed the crewmen and their next of
kin as they were still shown in Army records of June
1959. On the same date as the AP story, the Department
of Defense issued a statement through its Air Force
press desk in answer to the inquiry of a Washington
newspaper reporter:

A two-man team from the Army Mortuary Service
with headquarters at Frankfurt, Germany, departed on
May 11 to investigate the crashed B-24 in Libya reported by Gordon Dowerman [sic] of D'Arcy Exploration Co., Ltd. The B-24 had taken off from Soluch,

Libya, on 4 April 1943 on a high-altitude bombing
mission to Naples, Italy. Course of the flight is not indicated, nor if it actually reached its target. The Mortuary Team made a one-hour flight over the area and
plans a ground search as most feasible. Wreckage was
located about 158 nautical miles north-northeast of
Cufra Oasis.

The Army Adjutant General's office in Washington
had already wired the news of the bomber to all of the
next of kin listed in its records. News reporters in local
communities, alerted by news-wire reports, began ham-
mering away at those relatives they could locate, seek-
ing recollections, comments, and photographs of the
individual crewmen.

The surprising news had brought varying reactions
from the relatives.

Mrs. Emerson, sister of co-pilot Toner, probably ex-
pressed the feelings of many of them when she said she
had still not given up hope. "Maybe he's still alive
somewhere," she said.

Her last letter from Toner, when he had been overseas only two weeks, had said that he was about to go on
his first combat mission. "You live day by day here,
and no future," he wrote.

The pilot's wife, Amelia Hatton, had long since remarried and was now living in Illinois. Members of the
Hatton family said that the lieutenant had been reported missing in action on April 4, 1943, and that he
had been declared dead a year later. "His widow, Ame-

lia, contacted all the families of the other crewmen,"
they said, "and each of the relatives wrote back and
forth. But nothing further was ever learned by any of
them."

Also remarried was Machine Gunner Adams' wife,
Dorothy May. Before Adams left for overseas in 1943,
Mrs. Adams had been expecting a baby. The baby,
Michael, then 16 years old when the news was received,
was living with his mother and stepfather. Michael was
the only child of any of the nine crew members, and he
and his mother felt a greater involvement in the news
than most.

None of the other six crewmen or Lieutenant Toner
had been married. But the news was, of course, equally
depressing to their close relatives.

Alex Woravka noted that his last communication
from his brother was a 1943 cable from Africa advising
the family: PLEASE DON'T WORRY. The next message
they had was from the War Department saying that
John Woravka was missing in action.

Legally, the men had been dead under provisions of
the Missing Persons Act since April 5, 1944—more than
fifteen years. Their personal affairs and government
indemnities had long since been settled, but even so
there had always been a tiny flame of hope among some
of the relatives. No one had ever reported seeing the
men killed, and their bodies had never been found.
There was always a bare chance.

Lieutenant Hatton's B-24 might as well have disappeared into clear air, so far as the government had told the next of kin. It seemed incredible to the relatives that no one in the War Department and no one in the men's overseas outfit could give them further details of what had happened. The stonewall silence with which their inquiries were met was suspicious—as though something dire were being held back from them. It was not possible that an airplane so huge, with nine men flying it, could simply vanish.

The lack of original information, coupled with the difficulty in getting immediate on-the-spot information from the Libyan Desert, brought scores of speculative news stories within a matter of days after the B-24 was found. These naturally echoed the relatives' own speculations. The effect of seeing their worst fears and best hopes in print served to confirm their original suspicions and to increase their concern almost intolerably.

Rumors first began in Libya itself. In Benghazi, where the ghost bomber had been based at nearby Soluch airfield, a tantalizingly plausible rumor started from vaguely identified "nomads." Newsmen in the vicinity reported the story back to the States: A 1943 Italian armored convoy had been observed by nomads who were traveling the desert on camels. The convoy, near the region where the B-24 had crashed, had met and captured eight or nine Americans. Five of them had died or were killed by the Italians and had been buried in the desert. Then the convoy had moved on with the remaining Americans as its prisoners.

This early story was quickly discounted on grounds

that the bomber had not crashed until April 4, 1943,
and that the Italians and Germans had been completely
swept out of the desert by General Montgomery's British Eighth Army in January 1943—three months earlier.

Several free-lance writers tried solving the mystery
for various publications before the basic facts of the
story could be learned. The more that was written, the
more the story became confused—and the first meager
facts available called for still more speculation. Military
researchers required more than a month to dig into
some 60 pounds of records scattered at four different
locations in the United States before a plausible, fact-
based account of what probably happened to the
bomber could be pieced together. Many of the aircrews
involved in the story in April 1943 had been killed
during the war, were still missing in action, or had left
the Army at the end of the war and could not readily
be located.

While facts gradually rose to the surface, writers
looked over the location of the crash as shown by the
rare and scantily detailed maps of the region. The
bomber was tantalizingly close to several permanent
oases: Gialo Oasis was 218 miles northwest; Tazerbo,
184 miles west-southwest; the Oases of Cufra, 135 miles
south-southwest; El Gezira, 120 miles southwest; Jarabub, 213 miles north-northeast; and Siwa, 201 miles
north-northeast.

Writers began to wonder if it were not possible that
traveling nomads might have rescued or captured the
crew during caravan trips across the plateau, and pos-

sibly still have the men in custody somewhere in the remote interior oasis—or perhaps they had even been sold into slavery deep in the trackless central African Sahara. Most news publications ignored this speculative line; it could not be verified, in addition to the fact that there had been absolutely no history of any such actions for many years.

Professional newsmen, accustomed to getting what they asked from the Pentagon, besieged Air Force press officers for the minimum details needed to write the story off. Editors were pressing to settle it once and for all. To get at the basic facts, one news-feature writer asked the following questions immediately after the first overnight-search party returned from a flight to the scene of the crash:

1. May I have a copy or photostat of any flight logs or other such records found with the B-24?
2. Was the bomber set on autopilot when found?
3. Who was the squadron commander, operations officer, executive officer and intelligence officer on April 4, 1943?
4. What was the number of the plane's squadron and group?
5. What was the exact date of the flight itself?
6. What was the exact take-off time of the mission?
7. Do records of the War Department indicate exactly when the B-24 was reported missing?
8. What time should the B-24 have landed at Soluch if it made the raid with the rest of its squadron?
9. What were the exact weather conditions at Soluch at the time the bomber was lost?

10. How many missions had the B-24 flown prior to its last flight? Had its crew shot down any enemy planes as indicated by markings on the fuselage?
11. How many missions had the crew flown?
12. Did on-the-scene searchers report any damage to the B-24 by antiaircraft fire or machine guns? Was there any old, patched damage?
13. Was there an emergency hand-operated-type radio in the B-24? If so, did it work?
14. Was the B-24's compass operable? Its radio compass?
15. Was the B-24's landing gear up or down when it was found?

After a world war and 16 years, many of these answers were extremely difficult to find. Yet the more reputable writers, such as the one who made this inquiry, were working at the story for the same reason as were the Air Force press officers: The lack of precise information was beginning to get intolerable to all concerned. The sooner the facts could be learned, the sooner speculative stories would cease tormenting editors, public information officers, and relatives of the lost men.

Days followed before even a minimum of factual information came to light. The ghost bomber in the desert began to achieve every element of a natural-suspense mystery story which was not going to be solved without singular efforts. Those efforts were just beginning to get underway at Wheelus Air Base, 790 miles from where the deserted bomber lay.

6

THE COMPLEX SYSTEM of U. S. military forces scattered at many locations in Europe and Africa had recognized, in early May 1959, the necessity for prompt investigation of the bomber case.

Both Air Force headquarters at Wiesbaden and the Army's Mortuary System, Europe at Frankfurt, were promptly in touch with their headquarters in Washington. Messages clicked over teletypes, and all headquarters agreed that the Army was the proper agency to investigate—even though none of its men with Mortuary System experience were located in Africa. The African portion of World War II had ended in mid-1943, and there had been little demand for the System's service on that continent for several years. Nevertheless, the Army was obligated to conduct such investigations, and had the necessary trained personnel.

Army Captain Myron C. Fuller, expert investigator for Mortuary System, Europe, and Wesley Neep, an anthropologist for the System, boarded an Air Force plane in Germany on May 11, 1959, and took off for Wheelus Air Base. These two men were assigned to set up a search operation in the desert where the bomber had crashed—their mission was to find the missing crewmen if possible.

Fuller and Neep were both seasoned in the conduct of searches for missing military personnel. They had completed many such cases in Europe, and Neep had led an Army search into the United Arab Republic (Egypt) in 1958 for similar purposes and had met with prompt success.

Upon arrival at Wheelus, Fuller and Neep first arranged an aerial reconnaissance flight over the area where the B-24 had been reported by Gordon Bowerman.

Major H. E. Hays, operations officer of the 58th Air Rescue Squadron stationed at Wheelus, flew the Army men over the desert for a close look. The flight out, the search for the wreckage, the location of the B-24 by exact longitude and latitude, and the flight back, required nine hours. The wrecked aircraft was easily identified from the air as a B-24; it was located where Bowerman said it would be and looked just about as he had described it.

By the time Hays, Fuller, and Neep returned, the identity of the B-24 and its crew had been established in Washington through a preliminary search—based on information provided by Bowerman—of old Army Air Force records.

Next in order of business was a detailed physical inspection of the B-24. To expedite this, another Wheelus operations officer, Major William F. Rubertus, a B-24 Liberator pilot during World War II, offered to fly the Mortuary men to the crash scene. Reconnaissance had established that the desert floor was smooth and pebbly, and Rubertus believed he could land a medium-weight twin-engined SC-47 (a World War II transport) there and take off again without trouble.

A geodetic-survey outfit based at Wheelus, the Army's 329th Engineer Detachment, also offered to fly a single-engine L-19 plane to the scene ahead of the SC-47 to check out a good landing area at low altitude and to ignite smoke flares to indicate wind direction for Rubertus' landing.

Both crews made the trip on May 26, 1959. Rubertus, Fuller and Neep were accompanied by Captain (Doctor) James M. Paule, an Air Force flight surgeon and a known expert on desert survival, who would contribute a medical assessment of the bomber crew's chances of having survived.

Army Lieutenant Griffin A. Marr flew the L-19 to the crash scene without incident and lighted the smoke flares. Then Rubertus set the SC-47 smoothly down on the desert floor. Crew and passengers piled out eagerly. The B-24 lay in the sand just as Bowerman had described her, in a state of preservation that almost defied belief.

In her fuselage, little was disturbed that was not located at the point where it had broken in two behind the wing when the bomber crash-landed. A thermos jug was found, still full of coffee which tasted almost freshly made. Packages of cigarettes were scattered about, with packs of chewing gum and emergency rations. Some of the crewmen's high-altitude clothing still hung neatly on hooks where the men had placed them 16 years earlier. But there were no parachutes aboard the aircraft, and strangely, there also were no Mae West life preservers—and the Gibson Girl emergency hand-cranked radio was missing.

The bomber's Pilot's Flight Log was discovered, neatly listing names, ranks and serial numbers of the crew—exactly the names Washington had listed missing. Even the Maintenance Inspection Record was properly completed through April 3, 1943—the day before the bomber's Naples mission. The flight log had not been filled out with details of the flight and the pilot's remarks about the airplane's mechanical condition, but this was not usually done until after landing.

As for the bomber herself, engine oil was still in the tanks—although the gasoline tanks were dry; three propellers were bent in positions that showed the engines dead and the propellers only windmilling when they hit the sand; the fourth propeller and engine were violently torn loose from the wing—proof that the engine was still running with the last fuel in the tanks when the plane came down. The still-mounted machine guns were flanked with belts of good .50 caliber ammunition; most of the flight instruments were unbroken; hydraulic fluid was still in the lines and in the landing-gear shock struts; and, incredibly, the nose wheel and one of the main landing wheels still had undamaged, fully inflated tires.

The bomber was not set on autopilot—which might seem normal for a bailout—but the Air Force pilots recalled that a B-24 could be trimmed to fly or glide hands-off, and the autopilots of 1943 were so notoriously unreliable that many pilots never used them. The bomb-bay doors were open, indicating that the crew had bailed out. There were no bombs in the bomb bay and there was, of course, no way to tell whether they had been dropped on their Naples target, discharged on the way to or from the target because of fuel shortage or engine trouble, or salvoed in the desert prior to the presumed bailout.

Other than the quite minimum crash damage, there was not a tear or hole in the bomber's skin—either new or repaired. It had either never seen combat or had been a mighty lucky airplane. There were none of the customary "bombs" painted on the nose to indicate the number of missions flown, and there were no Italian or German insignias to score the shooting down of any enemy aircraft. The B-24 had all the look of a brand-new 1943 model, except for its crash damage.

The first reaction of the men was that of complete bewilderment. Everything found added to, rather than helped solve, the mystery.

The SC-47 searchers carried complete desert-survival and camping gear, so the men picked a temporary camp site and stayed for two days, not content to return to Wheelus until they had carefully explored the surrounding area for any possible clues to the missing crew.

Fortunately for the impatient relatives of the B-24's crewmen, and for newsmen who had taken such interest in the story, the SC-47 passengers included Air Force Master Sergeant Wayne L. Woods, an information writer, and Army Private First Class Gilbert Hodney, a skilled photographer. Their assignments were a precise narrative and full pictorial information on the bomber and her crash. Wood's story and Hodney's photographs were released to news media a few days later. The photograph of the stricken bomber made the world familiar with her woefully inappropriate name.

To add to the mystery, a further disquieting fact was learned. The long-range liaison radio set in the S-47 conked out. Noticing that the *Lady Be Good* had exactly the same model, the crew chief and radio operator —primarily out of curiosity—removed it from the B-24 and installed it in their plane. They turned the switch, the tubes lit up, and the set began crackling. It worked perfectly! Obviously the *Lady* had not been lost because of radio failure—the liaison set was the longest-ranged and most effective air-borne radio in Air Corps use in 1943.

Another fact that heightened the investigators' problem was the B-24's magnetic compasses. Both worked perfectly—as did the radio compass (or automatic direction finder).

A final look at the bomber's insides revealed oxygen bottles still roughly two-thirds full. There was no evidence of fire, and the CO_2 fire extinguishers worked properly when tried. Even the Very pistol recognition flares still fired on first try. In short, each discovered fact served only to cloak the mystery more completely.

There was no slightest evidence that any of the crew had found their bomber after landing. Everything pointed toward the men having parachuted, but even this was speculation. If they had parachuted, where had they jumped out? Nearby? A hundred miles away?

In low flights around the area nothing had been seen which looked in any way significant. After walking themselves footsore, the inspection party had found not one additional clue. The *Lady* had truly become a ghost bomber; she went on stubbornly refusing to give up her secrets. After two fruitless days the men gave up and returned to Wheelus. They had found out just enough to thoroughly confuse everyone concerned with the search.

It was clear that more strenuous efforts must be made if this story were ever to be fathomed. The Mortuary men decided to organize a systematic ground search.

They would need C-47 supply planes, many supplies of all types, a group of volunteer searchers, ground vehicles that could traverse desert dunes, and plenty of experienced desert people.

In Tripoli, Captain Fuller was able to get the services of Alexander Karadzic, a former Yugoslav Air Force and British Royal Air Force navigator who headed the Saly Company of Libya—a salvage and land-mine-removal outfit. Karadzic contracted to set up a desert "base camp" from which searchers could operate. He would also furnish desert vehicles, get an overland convoy to the crash site, and lend his expert advice.

Nothing of such scope had ever been attempted in the Sahara. The Air Force at Wheelus would provide large-scale airlift and supplies, and the Army Engineer detachment would furnish light planes as well as two-place H-13 helicopters—if anyone could find a way to get the short-ranged whirlybirds out to the crash site.

The overland convoy was ready to roll. Six nerve-racking weeks had gone into readying the strange air-ground operation for its unprecedented task. And during those weeks the public-information office at Wheelus had been flooded with inquiries from the United States about the ghost bomber and her crew.

During the organizing of the expedition, Memorial Day—May 30, 1959—came around, and with it the Wheelus Air Base's annual formal celebration. The observance was held at the Old Protestant Cemetery in

Tripoli where five sailors of an earlier America were buried. They had been killed when the U.S.S. *Intrepid* exploded prematurely in August 1804, just as it was being sent into Tripoli harbor loaded with gunpowder to set fire to the Barbary pirate fleet.

At the same time, a delegation of Air Force personnel from Wheelus had flown to Tunis to conduct a Memorial Day ceremony at the North Africa American Cemetery. Not especially noticed, while this was going on, was the North African Memorial Wall bearing the names of some 2,800 Americans killed or missing during the African campaign of World War II. Among the names were those of the nine lost crewmen of the *Lady Be Good,* and on the memorial was inscribed: HONOR TO THEM THAT TROD THE PATH OF HONOR. The service could hardly have been conducted at a more fitting time for Lieutenant Hatton and his crewmen.

7

CAPTAIN FULLER'S EXPEDITION was ready to leave Wheelus by mid-July 1959.

On the 17th, Major Rubertus again flew the Mortuary System people to the desert in an overage SC-47.

Desert expert Karadzic, with his overland convoy, was already several days en route. The rolling outfit, operated by Libyans trained to desert conditions, soon joined up with the air-borne party on the plateau.

In short order the ground party set up a temporary base camp just north of the *Lady Be Good,* and the operation was under way. The searchers assumed that the *Lady*'s crewmen—if they had parachuted shortly before the bomber crashed, which was thought likely—would have tried to walk out in the direction they had come from. It seemed safe to guess that they had bailed out north or north-northwest of where their plane came down. The first search would be in the immediate vicinity of the bomber—a couple of miles in all directions—and if nothing was found, they would then head north through the plateau.

With desert-worthy trucks the ground could be covered thoroughly. The men piled in their trucks and began scanning the plateau floor around the *Lady*. After some hours had produced nothing new, the party headed north in a wide front.

After about eight miles, the east end of the search line came abruptly upon the quite discernible tracks of five heavy military-type vehicles, heading north-northwest. The weight of the vehicles, years ago apparently, had pressed the loose pebbles down into the shallow sand, and the resultant slight ruts had gradually filled with fine, blowing drift sand so that the tracks were as easily followed from the ground as a country road—even though they had not been visible from the air. Word was passed westward down the line, and the men converged on the trail for consultation.

Fuller and Karadzic decided to follow the tracks, which Karadzic identified as Italian military-vehicle treads, along both sides, reasoning that if the *Lady*'s crewmen had fallen anywhere in the vicinity they probably would have found the tracks. Since the tracks were Italian, the trail must have been there when the men parachuted—three months after the last Axis forces had been swept out of Libya. And if the *Lady*'s men had found the tracks, it would seem logical that they would follow the trail back in the direction they had come from, hoping they were headed for an oasis or a village.

Two miles farther along came the first find. A pair of sun-dried, peeling U. S. aircrew high-altitude boots standing forlornly in the shallow sand! They were obviously many years old, and it was inconceivable that any other Americans but the Hatton crew could have shed them there.

"Look!" one of the searchers shouted. "They're purposely weighted down with pebbles. And put with the toes touching each other and the heels apart, to form an arrow pointing north!"

The man was right. But the marker was on the east side of the trail, and if the men had followed the direction the boots pointed, they would have missed the Italian tracks. The searchers decided to gamble on the fact that the men might have spread out after they parachuted and would probably have found the trail just as the search party had. For that matter, there was no way to tell whether the boots represented one of the *Lady*'s crewmen, two, or all nine of them. They may have scattered all over the plateau.

Instead of going north as the boots pointed, the searchers continued north-northwest up the vehicle tracks, spreading out on each side as before. At least they now knew that one, or some, of the B-24's crew had parachuted onto the plateau. Despite the almost unbearable heat, the party pressed on with renewed optimism.

The searing sun had brought out the weirdest possible array of makeshift gear for protection. They wore combinations of pajama shirts, short trousers, pith helmets, sunglasses, American helmet liners, silk-scarf turbans, handkerchief neck-protectors, canvas shoes—in short, anything that might shield the skin from the sun.

Moving forward along each side of the vehicle tracks, more and more slowly as the afternoon grew hotter, the men saw no signs whatever as they gradually worked to the north-northwest. The sun's rays were wilting, and the temperature zoomed to a measured 130 degrees Fahrenheit. If there was any humidity it was certainly not evident. A man's exposed skin dried like leather, and sand dust stuck to the dry skin and whiskers like adhesive abrasive, too eroding to brush off without the aid of water. Fortunately the convoy had plenty of water, but this fact led to guilty conjecture on the misery the *Lady*'s crew must have known 16 years before, after having been on foot in the desert the same length of time with neither water nor food.

The trapped men, reasoned the searchers, could only have had whatever water a few of them might have carried in canteens strapped around their waists—if indeed any of them had been so equipped, and if the sharp whiplash of the opening parachutes had not torn the canteens loose and thrown them straight to the desert floor, far from where the parachutes drifted to the ground. It was also obvious that none of the crewmen had reached the *Lady* after she came to earth. Not only because the supplies were untouched, but the distance from the boots marker was too great for the crew to have possibly seen where the bomber crashed, even if it had parachuted in broad daylight.

The desert sun sank almost instantly at nightfall, so the safari stopped and pitched camp well before dark. Once the sun disappeared, the air turned cold—so cold that the searchers were soon grateful for their adequate supplies of warm clothing. Off came the improvised sun shields in favor of heavier wrappings. The men shivered through the near-freezing night, their bodies unaccustomed to so sharp and rapid a temperature change.

Morning came as suddenly as night, and after a hasty breakfast the group climbed aboard its trucks and pushed on up the Italian vehicle tracks, fanning out on both sides. Suddenly one of the drivers stopped and began yelling.

"Another marker! Another marker!"

The second arrow marker lay in the sand alongside the western edge of the tracks. This one was made with strips of parachute weighted down carefully with large pebbles, and pointing directly up the trail to the north-northwest. The wandering men had found the tracks after all!

Again the searchers were fired with the enthusiasm of discovery. Leaving the marker undisturbed, they set off up the tracks again, looking eagerly along both sides

—close to the tracks this time and fanning out very little.

Farther up the trail six discarded Mae West life preservers were found. Beyond reasonable doubt, at least six of the crew had gotten together after bailout.

Each of the sun-bleached once-yellow life jackets had at least one of its two carbon-dioxide inflation cartridges punctured. The *Lady*'s crew had thought it was parachuting over water! This proved another thing: The bailout had been made at night when the surface below could not be seen.

Two of the jackets were clearly linked to the *Lady Be Good*. The names, stenciled in black ink were: WOR-AVKA and RIPSLINGER.

While this did not necessarily mean that the six who had thrown away the life jackets included Woravka and Ripslinger—there had probably been a first-come-first-served grabbing in the rush and confusion of parachuting—there was no longer any doubt that the searchers were headed in the right direction. It was also clear that the lost crew had been exhausted by the time they reached this point, because they had begun to discard useless equipment.

Keeping to the vehicle tracks, steadily north-northwest, the searchers found more parachute-made arrows at regular intervals, still pointing ahead along the trail. It was evident that the *Lady*'s crew had followed tight desert-survival discipline up to this point. Nothing had been found discarded that would have aided them in

Crew of the B-24 *Lady Be Good*. From the left: 1st Lt. William J. Hatton, pilot; 2nd Lt. Robert F. Toner, copilot; 2nd Lt. Dp Hays, navigator; 2nd Lt. John S. Woravka, bombardier; Tech. Sgt. Harold S. Ripslinger, engineer; Tech. Sgt. Robert E. LaMotte, radio operator; Staff Sgt. Guy E. Shelley, gunner; Staff Sgt. Vernon L. Moore, gunner; and Staff Sgt. Samuel R. Adams, gunner.

Two of the *Lady Be Good*'s officers sight-seeing at the Sphinx and the Great Pyramid near Cairo; Lt. Hatton on the left, and Lt. Hays on the right. With them was Capt. Martin R. Walsh, who led the bombing group on what was to be the *Lady*'s last flight.

The *Lady Be Good,* as it was discovered in the Libyan Desert sixteen years after crash-landing there. Damaged by the impact, the plane was otherwise almost perfectly preserved.

Holes in the nose glass were made by military inspectors to allow "cool" 120-degree outside air to enter the ovenlike fuselage.

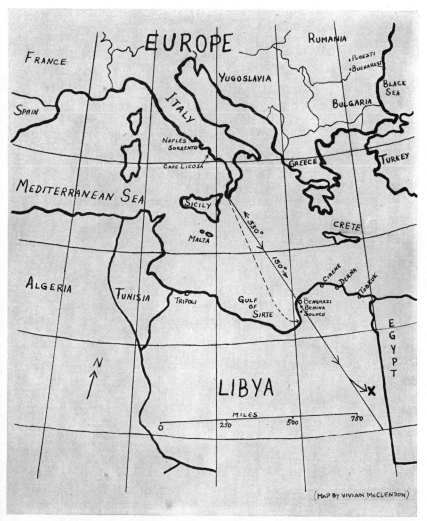

Map showing route actually followed by the *Lady Be Good* from Italy, passing directly over its home base at Soluch, ending in the Libyan Desert 450 miles in the opposite direction (x). Dotted line is the route crew thought it was flying.

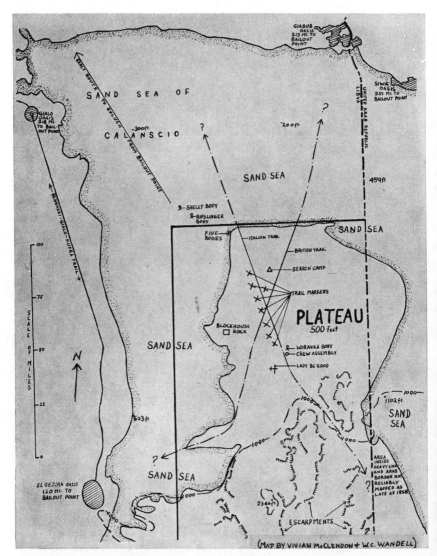

Area map showing crash site of the *Lady Be Good* and the points at which eight of the nine crewmen's bodies were recovered sixteen or more years later. Cross marks indicate trail markers left by survivors in their trek northward. Solid and hatched lines represent heavy military vehicle tracks mistakenly followed by men in search of aid.

Capt. Myron C. Fuller, Army search chief, points to parachute strip marker left by *Lady Be Good* crewmen to indicate direction they had taken. Looking on is Maj. Gen. H. R. Spicer, then commander of the U. S. 17th Air Force.

A 2nd Lt.'s flight cap, gold bar still in place, was among personal items discovered near the first five bodies found in the sand. In the background is an empty water canteen.

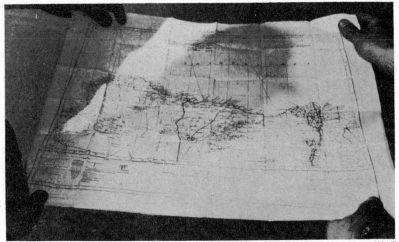

Perfectly preserved silk "escape" map used by crewmen of the *Lady Be Good*. Tracks on map may have led them to believe they were 100 miles north of the position where they parachuted from their bomber.

Pages from Sgt. Ripslinger's diary, begun on morning crew reassembled following bailout, later recovered intact and legible. First words entered, "All but Woravka met this A.M. Waited awhile and started walking." Six days later he recorded, "Palm Sun. Still struggling to get out of dunes and find water."

Rear view of the *Lady*'s broken main section.

Beneath one of the *Lady Be Good*'s engines stand Air Force searchers Capt. R. W. Pinkston and Airman 1st Class J. M. Meadors. Uniforms gave way to pajamas and Arab-style clothing in the intense daytime desert heat.

Aerial view of part of the dreaded Sand Sea of Calanscio surrounding the plateau on which the *Lady Be Good* was discovered. Dunes are as much as 700 feet high, and the sand so loose that a man will sink to knee depth with each step.

Oil exploration truck taking seismic soundings in the Libyan Desert in the area of the *Lady Be Good* crash site.

their attempt to live; and the methodical logic and placement of the markers indicated that someone was in good psychological control of the men. The abundant use of parachute cloths proved that the men had remembered their survival courses back in the States:

> After bailout, the light rayon cloth of your parachute should be retained above everything except food and water. The cloth weighs little, and it can serve many purposes. If you are in the tropics, it can shelter you from the rays of the sun, either as headgear or as a lean-to shelter, and it can be used to catch precious rain, or to soak up dew which can be squeezed into the mouth from the cloth. The cloth also can be used to make larger-than-man panels along the ground to be sure the search plane sees you when it goes overhead.

The instructions for using parachutes to catch water must have sounded over and over, mockingly, to the lost crew by this time. In this part of the Sahara there was no dew, and no one had ever heard of it raining here. Yet the parachutes had served a seemingly valuable purpose as markers, and undoubtedly they had used the cloth effectively as protection against the sun and from the cold at night.

Captain James Paule, the survival-expert flight surgeon, felt that the searchers would come upon the bodies of the crewmen at almost any time.

"Without water," he said, "the men normally could not last more than one day in this heat—two days at the outside, even with all the water they could carry. Remember, they were on foot—not riding in trucks. As far as distance goes, I would say they would be fortunate to cover twenty-five miles."

The searchers passed 20 miles from the original parachute marker on the trail. This distance, added to whatever distance the men had walked from where they had bailed out, must be right up to the men's maximum of 25 miles. Surely none of the searchers felt like doubting Doctor Paule. Some of them knew they couldn't have made 15 miles on foot, much less 25.

Slowly the big trucks moved on up the trail. Then those on the west side stopped. Before they could yell across at the drivers on the east side, those, too, had halted.

They had come to a cross-trail that must have been a real heartbreaker to the lost aircrew—if the tracks were there in April 1943.

Karadzic examined the tracks closely. They came from the north-northeast—probably from or to Jarabub or Siwa Oasis. The Yugoslav said they were made by 79 British vehicles. (Later research uncovered reports of a British convoy of about that size that joined up with Free French forces in December 1940, after France had fallen to the Axis, in the far south Tibesti Mountains' area north of the Free French stronghold at Lake Tchad, in French Equatorial Africa. The convoy might well have taken this route south-southwest at that time and it might also have attacked and demolished the meager Italian garrison at El Gezira Oasis—140 miles southwest—or the fort at the Cufra Oases—160 miles south—while en route to the mountains.) Karadzic figured that the tracks were at least as old as the Italian trail, and this was logical. The fighting in this area had been over for several months before the *Lady Be Good* came to the plateau.

Here was a problem. Which track would the lost crewmen have taken? The British tracks must have looked like a freeway to the men, in comparison to the five tracks they had been following. Then again, the Italian tracks led back in the direction from which the *Lady* had flown into the desert. Still the British tracks— on a heading of 15 degrees—must have seemed to come more directly from the coastal area. Not knowing how far south they were, and growing weaker, the men must have faced a terrible decision—a crossroad's decision that they might well have believed to mean life or death.

Assuming that the crewmen had already committed themselves to the Italian heading and would doggedly follow it at this stage of weakness, the searchers decided to pitch camp for the night, send a small force back for supplies, and move their base camp north from the *Lady Be Good,* and search the Italian trail farther in the morning. As they were settling in, one of the men discovered another parachute marker several hundred yards up the Italian trail and pointing along it as predicted. That settled the issue.

The next morning, several miles along the trail, there was another cloth marker. The endurance of this lost crew had been unbelievable. This marker was just as carefully made as the previous ones, and just as methodically weighted with pebbles. The crew must have walked more than thirty miles, and still been going —somehow.

A sixth and seventh marker were found on the same day, the last at least forty miles from where the crew had probably started walking. But beyond the seventh marker there was nothing. This was undoubtedly the last, and with the cloth-arrow the searchers found a pathetic piece of parachute cloth, cut to fit the face, with narrow eye slits cut out and the remainder evidently intended to serve as a sun-and-sand shield.

Fuller and Karadzic were sure the men must have died somewhere in the vicinity of the last marker, so again the convoy began circling. The two leaders laid out an orderly pattern around the marker, assigned each truck driver an exact search area, and loaded the trucks down with Army and Air Force volunteers to do the looking. An area of several miles in diameter was thoroughly combed. Not a single new item was discovered.

Next, the Italian trail was searched until it disappeared into the dunes of the Sand Sea of Calanscio, more than twenty miles beyond the seventh trail marker. Still nothing.

Fuller decided to set up a base camp in between the
Italian and British trails and conduct a minute examination of the whole northern end of the plateau. The
bodies *had* to be somewhere in that area.

While Fuller's new plan was still being worked out
with Karadzic and the truck drivers, one of the men
found an eighth marker. With this was another discarded Mae West, the seventh, and an airman's flight
helmet. To everyone's dismay, the marker was on the
west side of the British trail, pointing north-northeast
along the tracks. This must mean that the men had
split at the track's intersection—one party taking the
Italian and the other the British trail. The search really
became complicated then. The bodies of the crewmen
would probably be found at two different locations.

Fuller's new camp was set up 45 miles due north of
the *Lady Be Good,* right between the two sets of tracks
and past the intersection. The Mortuary System captain set up a search pattern for Karadzic's drivers that
covered more than 1,000 square miles.

Karadzic's desert vehicles were equipped with locally
designed sun compasses, mounted on the engine hoods
of the trucks. The Libyan drivers and the Army and
Air Force volunteer searchers worked with pairs of
trucks to cover the large area. The first truck of the pair
held to a steady course, using the sun compass for direction, while the second followed at a faster speed, zig-
zagging from side to side. With such a meticulous

pattern, the men felt they could not possibly miss anything on the plateau floor. They would have covered every square foot with at least one set of eyes.

But when the 1,000-plus square miles had been covered, not a single additional find had been made. It was as though the big bomber's crew had simply vanished.

To the searchers, it had not seemed humanly possible that the crew could have gone as far as the seventh marker. They marveled at the feat. Subjected as they had been, for over two weeks, to the scalding, baking sun, and half blind from the intense glare, even with sunglasses, they could hardly believe their own evidence. Even if the lost crew had not burned up and dehydrated during the day, it seemed that, especially after they had weakened, the men would have suffered horribly during the frigid desert nights. But where could they have stopped to die?

Suspense grew. At first the searchers had the uneasy feeling that their logic had misled them—that they were somehow looking in the wrong area. But gradually the conviction grew that the lost men—although it would have sounded incredible two weeks earlier—had followed either the Italian or British trails, or both, into the dunes of the dreaded Sand Sea. This would have required another 25 miles past the last marker on the Italian trail and about the same total distance along the British trail—a seemingly impossible 65 miles, just to reach the dunes. The crew must have had invincible courage and stamina to accomplish this fantastic hike. At least it was now certain that the lost men's bodies would never be found in the north-central part of the plateau. Absolutely nothing could have escaped the searchers in that area.

The party was beginning to look ridiculous to military people away from the desert and to news reporters as well. It had been more than three months since the crashed bomber had first been reported to the Air Force. The pitiful clues in the desert cried aloud for a final solution.

Walrus-mustached Major General H. R. Spicer, Commander of the U. S. 17th Air Force (then at Wheelus Air Base), may have been affected by the suspense too.

Perhaps General Spicer felt the pathos of the forlorn crew more than most. As a defiant ranking prisoner of the Germans during the early 1940's, Spicer had known many days of solitary confinement for refusing to discipline his fellow prisoners as the Germans wished, and for refusing to order them to cease making attempts to escape. Indeed, Spicer had been scheduled to be executed by a firing squad for his continued defiance of his captors on the very morning that the Russian army broke through and liberated his camp. Spicer looked hard and talked hard, but his record indicated a feeling of community with those in uniform who would, or had, sacrificed everything for a cause.

Spicer flew from Wheelus to the desert himself during the last days of July. Like most who had not participated in the futile search, he probably felt that an all-out effort had not been made. He checked maps and clues with Fuller and Karadzic and questioned the searchers in great detail, but in the end he, too, was satisfied that the *Lady Be Good*'s crew must have done the impossible. They must have walked into the dunes before they died.

The general joined a convoy of vehicles to search the dunes themselves. The convoy covered a total of 168 miles along both the Italian and British tracks, into the dunes and in between.

Then General Spicer also became frustrated.

In early August, he called on his headquarters at Wiesbaden for further assistance to the Army team. By midmonth that assistance was on its way down from Europe in the form of a huge Air Force 4-engined C-130 Hercules turboprop transport built to land on rough terrain regardless of its more than 100,000 pounds of weight. It belonged to the Air Force's 322nd Air Division at Évreux Air Base, France, and was coming down to airlift the 329th Army Engineer Detachment's two small H-13 helicopters to the *Lady Be Good*'s distant desert plateau. Special arrangements were made with the Libyan Government to allow the C-130 to use modern Benina Airport at Benghazi. Benina was almost half again as close as Wheelus to the desert plateau, and the C-130 could carry more cargo and require less fuel for the shorter flight.

The C-130 landed at Tripoli, loaded the two helicopters, flew to Benghazi, refueled, and went directly to the plateau search camp—some 410 miles south.

The big turboprop thumped heavily down on the plateau with its two Army whirlybirds and a load of supplies and fuel on a Sunday afternoon in mid-August. A second supply trip was made via Benghazi. Then the search really became intensified.

The Army H-13s covered large areas of desert terrain in a relatively short time, searching the fringes of the Calanscio Sand Sea in detail. But even the helicopters' eagle-eyed pilots and observers failed to find new clues.

In a final ultramodern effort, General Spicer succeeded in getting two RB-66 jet reconnaissance bombers flown down on a "training mission" from the Air Force's 10th Tactical Reconnaissance Wing at Spangdahlem Air Base, Germany. The RB-66s took aerial strip photographs of the entire area of the plateau in the north and of the several miles of Sand Sea that bordered the plateau. Yet, when the reams of photo-strips were developed, the result was the same: Nothing new.

The hard-working searchers had made one additional and tragic find, which, while not directly related to the lost crewmen, nonetheless gave a harsh indication of what probably had happened to them.

In their interminable sweeps across the arid plateau, they had come upon the body of an Arab nomad and his five camels. The man's body and those of the camels were practically petrified. The natural moisture in the bodies had quickly evaporated after death, and in an area where even the simplest bacteria could not live, the flesh had not decayed but had dried hard as leather and shrunk to fit the skeletons. It was conceivable that a person who had known the man in life could have recognized him—but it was most unlikely that any friend of the desert traveler was still living. Wesley Neep estimated that the man and his camels had died around 75 years earlier. This estimate was based largely upon goods and equipment found with the bodies. Every element of the one-man caravan's equipment lay just as it had fallen, completely untouched over the long years. Since the bodies were on the pebble-surfaced plateau itself, the scarce drift sand had not covered anything completely. The small amount of loose sand present had blown and eddied with passing desert wind currents, filling depressions and crevices and making smooth slopes against the sides of the bodies which had been turned against the random winds.

The mystery of the lost *Lady Be Good* crewmen had become almost maddening to the heat-baked searchers. Every possible means had been exploited to find the bodies, yet the desert would not give them up. By now top-flight writers and newsmen had made several trips to the forlorn plateau in supply planes. Eventually everyone—Libyans, Army, Air Force and journalists—decided that the crewmen had made it to the sand dunes of Calanscio and were forever lost in its cubic miles of changing, shifting sand.

Fuller and Karadzic finally decided to call off further searches. They felt that every possible effort to find the men had been made. All that could be done had been done. Only by the most improbable coincidence were the crew members likely to be discovered now. At least the evidence found had conclusively stopped the wild, speculative rumors. The place where their bodies were probably entombed was established, and there was no one left who had the slightest hope that they could have survived. The military vehicle tracks were definitely established as having been made before the men were lost, and there was no verifiable record of visitors to the area after the vehicles had passed through.

In his thoroughness, Captain Fuller had even checked out the early Benghazi rumor about an Italian convoy burying American bodies in the area—especially after Karadzic identified the one set of tracks on the plateau as Italian. About this special check, Fuller's assistant, Wesley Neep, wrote to a relative of one of the *Lady Be Good* crewmen:

> The story concerning the approximately 10 bodies [this was the way Fuller heard it] seen in the area of 3

abandoned Italian trucks has been misquoted considerably. This story is based solely on a report made by a traveling Bedouin who claims he drove his camels by these vehicles and saw the bodies. There is no indication these remains were ever buried, and no one else ever saw this scene. One 2½-day probe was made into this area by light vehicle, but with no success due to the very soft sand encountered. Another probe and search by helicopter and vehicle was made later covering the 340-degree route [the five Italian vehicles] right through the Sand Sea and some 20 miles to either side, but no trace was found of the abandoned vehicles.

In all, Neep wrote, his people covered 5,500 square miles in their detailed searches of the plateau and the surrounding Sand Sea. He concluded:

It is evident that the men walked out of the gravel plain and into the dunes of the Sand Sea. Once in this region they would begin to dig down into the sand for protection from the intense heat, and then be gradually covered with sand when unable to rise and continue walking.

Pat Frank, American writer who visited the plateau in August 1959, wrote touchingly of the crew in an article which appeared in *This Week* magazine on October 4, 1959:

"As I write this, it appears that the crew of the *Lady Be Good* did get to the Sand Sea, and that the desert has taken them, and holds them, and will always hold them."

The U. S. Army officially terminated its search after more than three months of demanding and expensive effort. Public interest then shifted back to the *Lady Be Good*'s last mission. No one could understand how the bomber, after flying 750 miles from the Naples area toward Soluch, could have continued on for 426 miles without its crew realizing it had overshot Soluch.

Although the evidence was then, and is now, based upon circumstantial inference, it had become possible to answer this question with a reasonable degree of certainty. Many of the clues in the desert served as a triple check upon earlier suppositions about the flight. Department of Defense press officers began working, in the late fall of 1959, with Robert E. Costello, producer of the Armstrong Circle Theatre television program, to try to fit the story together for the American people.

8

WHEN THE DRY DESERT SUN rose over East Libya the morning of April 4, 1943, a pink-painted B-24D—built to bomb and fight but never before flown in combat—sat with her pot belly hugging the sand. With the rest of the 376th Bomb Group's B-24s, she was "dispersed" to prevent a possible Luftwaffe surprise attack catching too many valuable bombers in an easy-target bunch.

The new B-24, just flown in from the States and checked out ready, had been named *Lady Be Good* by the crew which flew her over. Two days before, she had been scheduled for her first raid, but the ground force couldn't quite get the *Lady*'s miles of electrical and hydraulic lines, her four 1,200-horsepower engines, her radios and instruments to check out properly. So the *Lady*'s crew had left her in the sand and flown the

Group's beat-up old "spare" aircraft instead. Today she was groomed and ready for her debut over Axis-held territory. Her 514th Squadron number, 64, glistened in new paint on her nose.

But the *Lady's* rightful crew was in Malta. The old aircraft they had taken off in on April 2nd had had two engines go out during the mission, and they had been forced to land for repairs. So the newest plane in the Group was scheduled to make her maiden combat mission with the newest crew in the Squadron.

Hatton had flown the April 2nd mission as copilot to Richard Hurd in order to gain combat experience before taking his own crew out for its first try. The mission had not been much for learning. The B-24s were to bomb the harbor at Palermo and return to Soluch. When they reached Palermo, clouds completely covered the city and harbor—indeed covered the whole island of Sicily, including their alternate target. Without sufficient fuel to go elsewhere and drop their bombs on Axis targets, they returned to Soluch without contacting the enemy in any way.

Early in the morning of April 4th, after a breakfast of not-so-good British rations, Hatton, and his copilot Toner, Bombardier Woravka, and Navigator Hays washed their mess kits and returned them to their floppy sleeping tent. After carefully covering the clean mess kits and lashing all their meager possessions down, just in case of a *ghibli,* the officers attended a combat briefing staged on the sandswept airfield. Some of the crews sat on the sand and others on bomb crates, and got ready.

Colonel Compton, commander, was in charge. After a short pep talk, he turned the briefing over to the specialists—Operations and Intelligence.

Operations unveiled the map and revealed the mission: A high-level attack on Naples harbor at sunset. Three B-17 Groups from Algeria were going to plaster the area in midafternoon. It should be softened up by the time the 376th got there. Operations said that 25 planes were fit to make the trip, and that they would go in two sections. Since the mission was routine, Colonel Compton would not make it. Instead, Section A would be led by Major R. A. Soukup, and Section B by Captain Walsh. Then Operations called off the altitudes, check points, formation tactics and formation signals and sat down.

Intelligence briefed them on the ungodly concentration of ack-ack around Naples, but said that some of it should be out of commission when the 376th got there, because one of the B-17 Groups would have hit the same target by then. Intelligence also read off reports on the latest whereabouts of Italian and German fighters, how many, what types, and their latest tactics of attack.

The Group navigator read off courses, winds and expected weather and got all the crews to "hack" (set) watches with his own wrist watch—set by Greenwich time signal.

Then it was: "Let's go get 'em!"

Compton told them to be at aircraft in two hours —right after lunch, because the first B-24 had to start rolling at 1:15 local time.

Meanwhile, Hatton's radio operator LaMotte attended a separate briefing which brought him up to the minute on procedures for using his radio sets in emergency, on the latest German and Italian jamming techniques, and on how to help the navigator find himself if lost—which often happened, said the briefer. Finally LaMotte was given a sheet of paper which set forth the particular "colors-of-the-day," those Very-pistol flares to be fired for emergency recognition during each four-hour period of Greenwich mean time.

Ripslinger, the crew's flight engineer, and the rest of the team of enlisted men had gone out to the dispersal area early to get acquainted with the ground crew of their B-24. If they were going to be using somebody else's airplane, the men wanted to know all they could about it before take-off. During the morning, before a wind came up and began blowing sand in from the desert, Ripslinger and the three gunners had been helping the ground crew prepare the plane.

The ground-crew chief, Staff Sergeant D. L. Hendrickson, welcomed the help. Together the men removed the engine tarpaulins, drained the gas-tank filters, checked the shock struts, controls, propellers, machine guns, power turrets, and ran up the four Pratt-Whitney engines and checked the magnetos, oil, fuel and hydraulic pressures, generators, radios, and everything else on the long list. Then they loaded nine 500-pound bombs and saw to it that each gun and gun turret had a full load of ammunition and that all the belts were feeding properly. By eleven the new plane was ready to go. Since the sand was getting thick, the men put the tarps back on the engines before they went to chow.

All nine of Hatton's crew were at the *Lady Be Good*'s parking spot at twelve—a good hour early. Each man went to his crew position and checked the items he was responsible for.

Toner got the Pilot's Flight Log and filled it out, entering the name, rank, serial number and crew position of each of the men.

Hatton, by examining the Maintenance Inspection Record to see what kind of airplane they were getting, was able to determine that the *Lady Be Good* had flown only 158 hours since leaving the factory and had required very little maintenance since.

The bomber had undergone a 100-hour inspection only 5 flying hours earlier and had had her spark plugs and oil changed in the process. All four of the high-altitude engine superchargers were signed off as O. K. Her life rafts, fuselage, engine fire extinguishers and crew's safety belts had been checked properly and signed off. On March 25th, the bomber had been flown locally around Soluch for three hours, and her pilot had noted only that the intercom radio was cutting out at 28,000 feet, and that the oil pressure in No. 3 engine had fluctuated. But these malfunctions had been remedied, and Lieutenant Norman C. Appold had signed off the repairs after inspecting the work. The ground crew also noted that it had repaired the nose-ventilation hatch catch and the left main landing-gear safety switch and had done a small repair job on the top escape hatch —which had been slightly loose. The B-24 was officially pronounced ready to go.

Then the wind began to whip up. And the sand began to fly.

The Hatton crew went on about its business of making the *Lady Be Good* ready for flight. The ground crew took off the engine tarps at 12:45.

The two pilots checked the plane's normal rate of fuel consumption and fuel load. The bomber had 12 hours of fuel, maybe a little more, and the trip to Naples and back would take only 11 hours. It would be nice to have more fuel, but with 4,500 pounds of bombs this would mean overloading.

By the time the 25 Group bombers started engines, sand was blowing badly, and the whirling propellers— 100 of them, each hooked up to a 1,200-horsepower engine—added still more sand. Visibility on the ground was about zero.

All this sand, added to the boiling clouds blown downwind as each bomber took off into the wind, gave the engine oil filters a job they were never designed for. The fine air-borne sand particles also seeped into the superchargers, the fuel lines, oxygen fittings, machine-gun mechanisms, and the instruments. It blew into the eyes, noses and lungs of the crew members. They had to leave windows and hatches open until take-off. The heat from the sun had turned the bombers into ovens.

The raid would go, anyway. This was the final in a one-two-three-four punch at the Naples area, and it was urgent to the Allies that all four raids hit their targets. Besides, "Compton's Liberandos" had their honor to uphold. The other three Naples raids were being delivered by their competitors in Algeria, with B-17 Flying Fortresses. And B-17 crews habitually swore by the capabilities of their bombers and themselves while swearing at the B-24 Liberators and their crews. The Liberandos could hardly let a little sandstorm affect their part in the raid—even though the B-17s were probably taking off in perfect weather.

At 1:30 take-off rolls began from the graded sand runway. The pattern called for each bomber to wait one minute after the bomber preceding him had taken off, so that propeller turbulence and sand would subside as much as possible.

One by one they rumbled off through the swirling sand until all 25 were in the air. The normal 25 minutes this should have required was stretched to 45 because of the increasingly dim visibility. Pilots of later planes had to take off on instruments until they rose above the sand clouds created upwind by the bombers in front. Each pilot waited on take-off until he could see the bomber ahead break through the lower dust level and begin his climb. Otherwise he might still be on the strip ahead but invisible in the sandstorm. Once up, visibility improved enough to see the other planes and get in formation.

A few long circles, and the 12 in Section A formed up and headed north. Gradually the 13 planes of Section B —which had had a double dose of sand—zoomed off the ground and into formation.

Hatton's *Lady Be Good* was the twenty-first plane to take off. He shook free of the low-level sand clouds and flew into position behind, and to the right of, Lieutenant E. J. Feely's B-24. Feely led the second flight of two elements (six B-24s) in Section B.

The first two elements of the Section were led by the Captain Walsh with whom Hatton and Hays had made the recent trip to Cairo. Walsh was a real old-timer with the 376th. He had begun operations with the Group when it was based at Fayid, Egypt, and had been awarded the Purple Heart after flying a mission from Palestine during which his B-24 had countered a head-on attack by a Luftwaffe Junkers-88. Hatton and the other newcomers in the Section must have felt fortunate to be flying behind such a veteran.

Soukup's Section A was several miles ahead, and several thousand feet higher than Section B, as it climbed out north-northwest on course for the toe of the Italian boot. The first section, not having been exposed to as much sand as the second, had little trouble on the flight. Only one B-24 of the twelve turned back to Soluch because of engine trouble, and this occurred a short time after take-off.

Section B, on the other hand, was literally plagued with sand-induced mechanical troubles. By 5 P.M. local time, three B-24s had fallen out and returned toward their home base. Section B was down to 10 bombers.

The ten, following several miles behind Section A, droned steadily over the tip of Italy at 25,000 feet preparatory to taking a diversionary westward course toward the island of Sardinia, to confuse Axis radar. At this altitude, without the electrically heated oxygen masks, gloves, boots, and flying suits of later days, it was just plain cold. The outside-air temperature was below freezing, and the crews rubbed their hands and stamped their feet to keep warm. Meanwhile, since they had entered enemy air, every crewman's eyes—especially those of Hatton's brand-new crew—scanned the skies for signs of enemy aircraft or antiaircraft bursts. All crewmen other than pilots and radio operators checked and rechecked their .50 caliber machine guns. All the men who would fire guns if attacked had shot off a few rounds after take-off, just to be sure the guns would work when needed. They were ready for business. The target was still more than an hour north. The big heavily loaded Liberators droned on, deadly in their solid formations.

But Section B was shot with bad luck on April 4, 1943.

At 6:40 P.M., Lieutenant F. W. Milam, leading the last flight in the Section, wagged his wings and peeled off from the formation. When he landed at Soluch, he reported:

"All my engines were rough, and it was hard to keep formation; then my Number Four prop ran away and I had to feather it. Couldn't keep up on three rough engines, so I had to come back."

At 6:45, Lieutenant K. P. Iverson, flying odd-number-four position in the leading flight of the Section, headed south.

"Both Number One and Number Four engines went out on me," he reported. "I could hardly stay in the air. Had to drop my bombs in the sea in order to get home."

Then at 7 P.M., the old veteran, Captain Walsh, dropped out.

"I couldn't get enough performance out of my engines to keep altitude and keep up the formation air speed," Walsh reported when he landed at Soluch.

However, Walsh did not give up easily. Alone once he left the formation, and deep in enemy territory, he struck out singlehandedly with his ailing plane to bomb the Group's alternate target—ancient Crotone, Italy. There he ran against a squall line of thunderstorms that completely obscured his target, but, sighting a freighter in the town's harbor, he dropped his string of bombs on it.

"My bombs straddled the freighter, with no hits observed," Walsh observed disgustedly to Intelligence.

The original Section B, now down to seven B-24s, still bored toward Sardinia at roughly 200 miles an hour. With 6 planes gone, the formation had seen some fancy juggling for new positions—and still more were to drop out. Section A had 11 of its original 12—which the tail-along B Section could see clearly ahead of them.

Shortly after Walsh dropped out, Hatton's element leader, Feely, began having trouble. By then they were deep in enemy air—past the volcanic island of Stromboli, off the Italian west coast in the Tyrrhenian Sea.

"First I lost Number Three supercharger," Feely told Intelligence debriefers. "I feathered the propeller, shut down the engine, and dropped my bombs to try to stay with the formation. I thought I would at least make it over the target with them, but then I lost a second engine and had to come home."

Six B-24s were left.

At 7:20 P.M., Lieutenant W. M. McCain, who had started out flying Walsh's right wing, was leading Section B's first flight of three planes—with Hatton flying McCain's right wing in No. 2 position.

Just as this new formation of six planes got settled into position, another pilot had trouble.

"My waist gunner's oxygen mask froze up," reported Lieutenant D. E. Lear. "The crew told me on intercom that he was unconscious, so I dove down to fourteen thousand feet to revive him. By the time he came around, I'd lost the formation, so I decided to go over to Crotone and see if I could get something out of the flight. I ran into severe turbulence, searchlights and antiaircraft fire," he said, "and my gyro blind-flight instruments went out in the middle of all this. Then flak hit my plane to boot, so I salvoed my bombs and came home."

Section B was down to five—for five more minutes.

At 7:25 McCain peeled out of formation and headed back. Like Lear before him, McCain had oxygen-mask trouble—with a waist gunner and his tail gunner at the same time. By that time daylight was beginning to fade. McCain figured his percentages and decided to head directly back to Libya.

Hatton, who had moved progressively forward until he was flying No. 2 position, presumably fell heir to lead position as soon as McCain moved out. Lieutenant Worley, one of the three remaining pilots, reported: ". . . I think the leader was number sixty-four."

The formation was then over Sorrento, about 16 miles south of Naples—roughly 5 minutes flying time. At this point, 7:45 P.M., the three pilots flying Hatton's wings reported that the sun had already been down (even at 25,000 feet) for 10 or 15 minutes. The ground below was in heavy shadow.

With daylight almost gone, and still several miles from his target, Lieutenant Hatton, leading his remnant little four-bomber formation, on his first combat mission, must have felt insignificant in the darkening

skies. There were only three B-24s left to help him attack the most heavily defended Axis bastion in southern
Europe. The only facts surviving the day, and not de-
pendent upon memory, are taken from the other three
pilots' reports to Intelligence officers after they landed.

Worley said that the formation leader turned south
over Sorrento because the target would be too dark to
bomb by the time the four planes got there. (This
might well have persuaded Hatton, who knew that if the
target was too dark to see in the Norden bombsight, he
might be dropping his bombs right into the middle of
a defenseless civilian city.)

Swarner reported that the "formation held together
until we broke up over Licosa [Cape Licosa, Italy] because of darkness." Swarner continued south and
dropped his bombs on the Catania airfield in Sicily. He
landed at Soluch at 10:45 P.M.

Gluck said merely that: "The formation leader
turned south away from the target and we followed
until darkness. We dropped our bombs on Catania
which was showing a landing beacon [probably to help
night-fighters or night-flying transports en route with
reinforcements to Tunisia find the airfield, which was
dangerously close to the foot of 10,250-foot Mount
Etna], and then we set a course for Soluch. When the
aircraft was dropped to a lower level at this time, the
engineer reported one hour of fuel left. We immediately set course for Malta, landing there at 10:45."

Worley dropped his bombs in the Mediterranean,

seeing no target in the dark, and returned to Soluch, landing at 11:10, the last on the ground of the 24 planes that got back safely from Naples.

At 12:12 A.M., the Benina Radio Direction Finder (RDF) Station received a call from Lieutenant Hatton in the *Lady Be Good*. Hatton asked for an inbound bearing to Benina, which was adjacent to the Soluch airfield. Benina operators cranked their loop antenna around until the voice count faded out. The operators read their scale: 330 degrees.

"Hello six four. Hello six four," called Benina (actually using code words for identification). "This is Benina RDF Homer. Your bearing is three-three-zero degrees magnetic from the station. Repeat. Bearing is three-three-zero. Over and out."

The *Lady Be Good* acknowledged the message and signed out, unaware that the plane was being sent deeper into the Libyan Desert—over which the crew had already been flying for the last few minutes.

A single RDF station in 1943, with its single rotating loop antenna, had no way of knowing whether an aircraft was inbound or outbound in a certain direction from the station. The "voice fade" told the operator only that the plane was along a certain straight line passing through the loop. Both the radio operator at the RDF station and the *Lady*'s crew had made a fatal mistake: Both had assumed that No. 64 was inbound to the station. Unless there had been a second RDF station several miles away—and there was none—to run a bearing at the same time with Benina, there was no way to be sure exactly where No. 64 was. Two stations could easily have fixed the plane's position: A line would be drawn in both directions on the map, through the center of each station, and the point where those lines crossed each other would be the location of the plane. Naturally, the lines would go farther and farther apart if extended in the wrong direction. Such a check was impossible at Benina-Soluch in April 1943. Plane crew and radio station had made a mistake known as "reading off the back of the loop."

The actual bearing from No. 64 to Benina at 12:12 A.M. April 5, 1943, was 150 degrees—the exact opposite of what both the station and Hatton must have thought it was. If at this time, or at any time within the preceding thirty or forty minutes, the *Lady Be Good*'s crew had tuned in its ADF (Automatic Direction Finder), they would almost positively have picked up the Benina beacon. The automatic pointer needle on the ADF would have pointed toward the station as they flew in from the Mediterranean, would have swung around as the B-24 passed the station, and would have pointed directly behind the plane as soon as it passed Benina. The ADF in *Lady Be Good* was working properly, and other pilots had no trouble picking up Benina beacon on their sets at the same time. The apparent answer to why the crew failed to use the ADF set is that they were confident that they knew where they were until they were out of range with the relatively weak ADF.

Lieutenant Hays, navigator on the *Lady,* must have consulted with his two pilots about the bearing—three-thirty degrees from the station, one-fifty degrees to the station. Just what he had them holding. Keep on that course, and start dropping down to low altitude in a few minutes. Should see the coast before long. Remember: It was a strong tail wind on the way up, so it's a strong head wind now. That's what's holding us up.

There was no way to tell wind direction in the dark except by checking time and distance against star positions, which took a lot of time and work. They probably had not done this. Why go to all that sweat when in a few minutes the plane would be close enough to the station to tune in the radio compass and follow the needle home? Surely no one had any reason to doubt the course he had given the pilots. Hadn't Benina just confirmed it to within a degree or two?

By this time, Hatton must have started easing the *Lady* down to lower altitude to be sure he would be able to spot the coast line when he crossed it. Except for Hays, Toner and Hatton, the rest of the crew was probably slumped down at crew positions catching some hard-earned shut-eye. Possibly LaMotte was still working with his radios, although there are no records of further calls from the *Lady.*

Hatton and Toner had undoubtedly been taking turns flying for the past hour or so—as soon as they were sure the plane had passed Malta, and there was no danger of Luftwaffe night fighters sneaking up from behind.

By one o'clock, the crew must have grown uneasy about its location. The radio compass was turned on, and, in addition to the pilots, Hays and LaMotte were probably taking turns trying to tune in the low-power beacon at Soluch from which they were long since out of range.

LaMotte probably kept trying again to reach Benina, but either he was out of range at low altitude or else the operators of the station had their receiver volume turned too low to pick up a call from so far away. By now, the *Lady* was at least 200 miles deep in the desert.

Could it be possible that the Jerries were nuisance-raiding the Benghazi area, and all the radios had been turned off? There was something odd. Well, hold the course. We'll get there before long and find out.

But 1:30 came, and still no coast line.

Go lower. We're getting low on fuel. Can't afford to miss the coast line when we cross it. Not enough fuel to muddle around.

Try turning twenty degrees to the left, just in case we've drifted off course a little to the west. We just might be flying over the Gulf of Sirte and already have passed Benghazi. Sure we should have been there by now.

Call Mayday to Benina. Keep calling. If we don't get there soon, we'll have to jump. Don't want to try to ditch this monster in the sea at night. B-Twenty-four's break in the middle during a ditching and sink like a rock. Remember?

Could we possibly have already crossed the coast? Could we be over the desert?

How could that be? We couldn't have missed the breakers. Been watching for them like hawks for almost two hours!

Well, something's wrong. Why won't Benina answer us?

Your guess is as good as mine. Maybe they're having an air raid.

By this time the entire crew must have been taking turns up front, peering out the windshield between the pilots.

Just in case, everybody, grab a Mae West and a chute and get strapped up. We've just about had it.

The seven nonpilots would have gotten into their life preservers and parachutes, as Toner and Hatton took turns flying the bomber and getting their emergency equipment on.

There goes the first red light. Out of fuel on Number One. Open the bomb bay doors and let's get out of this thing. Couldn't be very far from shore now. Don't forget to inflate your Mae West after the jump sack opens. There goes the red light on Number Three. Let's go, men. After you, Bob. I'll hold her steady till you get out.

As he floated down, Hatton must have felt that his

men were reasonably safe. They each had on a life preserver, the sea was warm, and the Group would surely
send out search planes at daylight and find them floating in the water.

The deserted *Lady Be Good* flew alone in the night
sky. Her altimeter and rate of descent showed she was
losing altitude rapidly, and she had not been very high
to begin with. She staggered on a few more miles, then
No. 2 engine gulped its last drops of fuel, and its propeller joined the two before it, windmilling. The rate of
descent increased rapidly, but she was still fairly level.
Lower. Lower.

Then, with her last engine turning mightily on its
last few cups of gasoline, the *Lady* smacked into the
desert. The running engine's propeller tore viciously
into the hard sand and out of its wing nacelle. The
tremendous jolt whirled the *Lady* in a half circle to the
east. Her fuselage snapped in two from the sudden
stress, and the two pieces of the almost-new bomber
settled heavily into the quiet deserted terrain. Sand
dust sifted over her. Everything again was still.

A few miles north of where the *Lady* came to rest,
her nine-man crew was on its way down. The instant
the men's feet touched sand instead of water, they must
have known what they had done wrong. At altitude,
they had had a strong tail wind instead of a head wind.
They had already over-flown Benina-Soluch, too high,
before they began looking for it. It was all very clear.
Now.

9

SHOUTING LUSTILY AS THEY DROPPED
through the cold dark air, the crew of the *Lady Be
Good* would be able to keep a semblance of contact
during the parachute rides to earth. As they fall, each
of the latter jumpers might hear the consoling yells of
the two or three others below and upwind of him.

"Remember," echoes a distant survival-instructor's
voice, "you must get out of that chute the instant you
touch the water, preferably slipping out of your harness
six or eight feet above the surface. Dive, and swim
underwater toward the wind as long as you can before
you come up. The wind will have blown the collapsing
canopy the other way, and you're sure to be out from
under the chute if you come out upwind of it. The
canopy will be wet, and air cannot come through. If
you come up under the chute, you're bound to drown."

But at night, how were you to tell which way the wind was blowing? And how would you know when to get out of the chute harness? You wouldn't know where the water was until you were in it. These frightening thoughts must have darted through the men's minds as they descended through the thin, cold darkness, readying themselves for fast action at the moment of impact.

Down. Down. *Hay-ay-ay!* Down some more. Yell again. Got to keep in voice contact. Have to stick together. Be easier to spot from the air as a group.

Thud! A jarring *whop,* and the first man crumples, rolling end over end in the sand. Then stillness.

Got to spill the canopy, one dimly remembers. I'm on solid ground, not in the water. Got to spill the canopy. Can't let the wind drag me over the ground. God, what a bang!

He tugs at his top shroud lines, collapsing the parachute canopy as it billows in the ground breeze. He gets up. There is no sound for a moment. It is pitch dark except for the stars.

What the devil? What is this? An island? Where am I anyway?

A fleeting sound of panic grips him. He feels abandoned. Alone. Then the alarm is gone. He hears a shout.

Hay-LO! Hay-LO, there. Where is everybody?

The first man almost laughs with relief. Then he feels silly, like a kid being scared of the dark.

Hel-LO! This way.

Within a minute or so the desert seems alive with

halloo's. Everyone begins running toward everyone
else so that the group first comes together in three or
four small batches. Perhaps then the pilot's voice.

Form up on me. I'll keep up the chatter so you can
find me. Hey! One, two, three, four. Hey! One, two,
three, four. Hey!

Slowly the men come together in the darkness, dragging their half-gathered parachutes, tripping and stumbling on the shroud lines. Closer. Then they are in a
group, slapping backs, yelling noisily in relief, bear-
hugging each other in the dark, shroud lines, parachutes and all, tripping over each other awkwardly. It
is good to be together and on the ground.

An authoritative voice. Roll call.

Toner.

Here!

Hays.

Ho!

Woravka.

Silence.

Woravka?

Silence.

Where's John?

No answer.

John?

Silence.

All right. *Ripslinger.*

Here, sir!

LaMotte.

Here!

Shelley.

Here, Chief!

Moore.

Here!

Adams.

Here.

All present and accounted for.

All but Woravka.

Where is John?

He doesn't answer.

Maybe he delayed a bit opening his chute and didn't drift as far as we did. The wind is blowing quite a bit.

He might be too far away to hear us.

Anybody got any emergency signal flares?

Yes. Several.

Light one and hold it up--high.

A crewman ignites a flare and holds it above his head, the flame arcs brightly against the darkness. Ears strain to hear. Someone clears his throat.

Shut up. We'll miss him.

Silence. Tingling silence.

Light up another.

A second flame splits the darkness. Then a third. Silence closes in from all directions.

Brother, he must be a long way off.

Must be. Have to look for him when it gets light. Sit down now and try to figure out how we came down. I came down from that direction, I think. Which way did you come after you hit?

I believe from that way.

Rip?

That way, sir.

Bob, how about you?

From over there, I think.

Okay. There's the North Star, in the direction from which we all came, apparently. Low, over there. Their eyes are now accustomed enough to the crisp starlight so that each man can see almost clearly.

John was one of the first to bail out. Must have come down somewhat north of them. In what order had he jumped?

He had been standing right over the bomb bay, and was the third man out.

Well, it began to make sense. Woravka might have been first to reach the ground. If so, he'd be farthest north. Maybe he delayed pulling the rip cord, besides going out early. In that case, this stiff wind wouldn't have carried him as far as it had the others. A few seconds would mean a lot of separation. Okay, that's logical. As soon as it's light they'd head north and look for John. He could be hurt, and unable to walk. Several of them had taken a hard thump on landing.

Brrrrr. It's cold.

The thing now was to try to figure out where in the devil they were. And to hold onto everything they had come down with. It was a cinch they were in the desert somewhere. This was no beach. They would need all the survival gear they had.

Some of them gratefully notice they still have on sweaters, flying boots, high-altitude jackets, and even high-altitude trousers. In the excitement of being lost and jumping, they hadn't really noticed until it started to get cold. The desert air was cutting now. The less heavily clad huddle in their parachute canopies for warmth.

They gather in a circle and begin talking.

Driest, coldest water they had ever seen, Lieutenant.

Yeah, and scratchy.

Strained laughter and muted chuckles.

How had they gotten over land?

Ask Lieutenant Hays. He's the navigator.

Not really sure. Must've picked up one awful tail wind somewhere. Couldn't tell where. Everybody remembers that sandstorm blowing off the desert when they took off. Usually those things lasted for days, so they were told. It only took five and a half hours going up to Naples, counting getting in formation, the climb up to twenty-five thousand feet with a load, and the diversionary course toward Sardinia after aborting. Would have sworn it'd be five, maybe five and a half hours coming back. The pilot thought so too.

Boy! Will they ever get the devil when they get back to camp. That B-twenty-four cost old Uncle Sugar about a quarter of a million dollars. Colonel Compton would probably have them in for a *personal* interview.

And wait'll Lieutenant Rose gets back from Malta and finds his own private-type airplane gone. He'd chew them but good. "Lady Be Good," he'd say. "Hah. Not much good, that Lady now, wherever she augered in!"

Almost hate to go back after this, to tell you the truth.

Okay, then, that's that for now. Let's roll up and get some sleep. Try to find a smooth spot in these rocks. They're only on the surface. Dig out hollows for your rear end and your shoulder blades. You'll sleep better if you fit yourself to the ground. Don't worry. The Group will have planes out tomorrow to find us. They're bound to dope out what we did wrong, and maybe what several other planes from the Group did too, though I hope not. There'll be a search tomorrow. They'll find us. Let's get some sleep now. We'll start walking back in the morning, just in case.

After a restless, shivering three-hour sleep, Toner, as the sudden light comes in the east, fishes around in the snap pocket of his jacket and removes his diary and pencil. The diary is a habit with him, and in a way reassuring. He wants to remember the details of this war, and there has been too much happening to try to store it all in his mind. He writes on the page marked Sunday, April 4, 1943:

Naples. 28 planes. Things pretty well mixed up. Got lost returning, out of gas, jumped, landed in desert at 2:00 in morning, no one badly hurt, can't find John, all others present.

Toner does not know it, but his diary containing this entry as well as others made later, will eventually be recovered.

The first rays of sunlight wake the others. There are groans and rubbings of protesting bones. That sand is hard and cold. Most of the men are stiff and sore.

Under Hatton's direction they take careful inventory. Most have pocket-size escape kits. In each are a few squares of concentrated candy, a pack of gum, an escape map, a compass, a hack-saw blade encased in rubber for insertion in the anus (to conceal the blade) if capture were likely, two concentrated chocolate bars, and some twenty-franc gold pieces. Most of the men have a pocket-size message from President Franklin D. Roosevelt to French, Italian, and Arab peoples, in each language, identifying the bearer as a member of the U. S. Armed Forces, offering a reward if the bearer is "guarded from harm" and "returned to the nearest Allied Forces." There is one canteen half filled with water, and each man has his parachute. Two of them have stale sandwiches (cadged from the mess tent before the mission) stuffed in their pockets. Some have hunting knives, and a few have sunglasses which had not been thrown loose when the parachutes opened. There are even two flashlights among them. They are in fair shape except for water. They figure they can keep going three or four days if they have to.

As far as sight carries, there is nothing but flat, barren sand except for one bleak square-looking rock looming up several miles northwest. In the south there is a dim line that could be hills. The Sahara Desert lay in that direction, they know, and for sure there were no hills around Benghazi and Soluch. To the west, north and east, nothing but sand and the one big rock. No *Lady Be Good,* no Lieutenant Woravka; just sand and more sand.

Ripslinger also remembers his diary. While the rest finish their outfitting job, he writes:

Sunday, April 4. Mission to Naples, Italy. T.O. 3:10 and droped [sic] *bombs at 10:00. Lost coming back. Bailed out at 2:10 A.M. on dessert* [sic].

Like Toner's, his diary will be found later.

Hatton, as first pilot and competent leader, sees to it that nothing is left behind that could be useful. The heavy parachute harnesses are cut loose from the shroud lines and thrown in a pile. Shroud lines are cut loose from canopies and stuffed in bulging pockets. The canopies themselves are folded neatly and draped around the men's shoulders—it is already getting hot and the rayon helps ward off the sun's stinging rays. Four men are allowed half of one of the two stale sandwiches, and the other four get a candy square each. They are all allowed to wet their tongues with water from the half-filled canteen, and issued a stick of chewing gum apiece.

They spread out, several hundred yards between each, and head north on a broad front to look for Woravka. They also watch strainingly for signs of their plane: it has water, coffee and food that might possibly have survived the crash.

Every now and then someone yells, "Hel-LO, John!"

There is no answer. The men examine every dark spot, search every depression in the sand. One of the crew decides his feet will never stand the heat of both GI shoes and flight boots, so he stops for a moment, takes off his boots, arranges them to look like an arrow pointing north, weights them against wind with large pebbles, and rejoins the line of searchers. There is still no sign of the bombardier. They have covered nearly a mile on a broad front. No John Woravka.

Then the most westerly of the men begin shouting through cupped hands at the others.

Tracks! Tracks! Tank tracks! There are tracks over here!

The word passes from man to man, and each one, as he hears the news, begins hurriedly to close in on the west end of the line.

Don't run! Save your strength. The tracks will still be there. Slow down, everybody!

Sure enough, there are tracks. Tracks left by five motorized vehicles of some sort. The men can see the tracks stretching away several miles.

North northwest! Pretty close to the heading they had figured to get them home. The tracks must go to Benghazi, with a little dogleg somewhere. Maybe they were not so bad off after all.

What about John?

No telling where he is. Unless he's way off up there, somewhere. Maybe he started walking back as soon as he hit. If he did, he must be heading the way they were, miles ahead. But they'd catch him, for sure.

Let's head up the trail.

There is a chorus of approval.

Slowly now, slowly in this hot sun. Don't work up more sweat than you have to. It'll use up your body water that much faster. Walk very easy and keep watching for B-Twenty-fours. If one comes near, we'll all spread out and wave our chutes like mad.

Foot after weary dragging foot they trudge. On and on up the trail, back in the direction of Soluch.

By midafternoon the heat is too much, even after frequent rest breaks. Not the slightest sound comes to the desert. There are no planes. There is nothing but hot sand and hot sun.

Rest? Sit down and broil your hindquarters? No, you have to rest standing up or squatting so that you can catch the slight whispers of horizontal air that wafts through the vertical columns of heat rising from the scorching sand.

Let's try holding up our chutes as shelters and sweat it out until this damned sun goes down some.

What kind of an idea is that? Hold them up how?

Weight down one end with rocks and hold the other end over your head.

Oh.

Good idea.

Yeah. Got to do something. This is awful.

The faltering column halts and sets slowly to work as best it can. Sections of the parachutes are spread against the western sun, and the west-facing edges are weighted with pebbles almost too hot to pick up. Then they crouch beneath the meager shelters, holding the east-facing edges of the cloths over their heads. It isn't much! They have to squat on their baking feet, but it is better than walking in the blistering sun. It is at least bearable.

Eight men, too exhausted to talk, hunch under their feeble sun shields, hating each succeeding breath that draws the searing desert air painfully into their lungs. They sit nearly motionless until the sun is almost down. No B-Twenty-fours have flown over, or even within earshot.

No telling which way they'll come looking for us. Might not come as far south as our plane crashed. We could be a good way north of it already. Hadn't we better leave markers every so often, big enough so they can be seen from the air?

Sure. Why not? Good idea.

The sun is beginning to disappear, and they can feel the heat leaving the desert. At first, when the temperature drops to 100 degrees, there is a sensation of chilliness. Achingly, they get to their feet and fold their parachute cloths. Toner writes:

Monday 5. Start walking N.W., still no John. a few rations, ½ canteen of water, 1 cap full per day. Sun fairly warm. good breeze from N.W. Nite very cold, no sleep. Rested & walked.

One of them suggests that each tear off a strip of parachute about a foot wide and two feet long. The white cloth ought to be visible from the air and they can make big arrows with the cloth, weighting the strips with stones so that the wind won't blow them away.

They pitch in, and soon a respectable arrow marker lies in the sand, neatly held down by large pebbles. It points north-northwest along the tracks they have been following.

Listen, men. From now on, we'll walk mostly at night. I know you're all beat, but we've got to get along toward Soluch. Even a few miles might mean the difference between being found or not. We may be farther out than we think. If we're closer than we've guessed, we might make it under our own power, if we're careful and don't overexert ourselves. Maybe Group looked for us in the sea today, in which case they'll search the desert tomorrow. Now, everybody, take exactly one canteen capful of water and one candy square. Then we'll sit still a few minutes and look at our maps again before we start out.

Ripslinger writes in his diary:

Monday, April 5. All but Woravka met this A.M. Waited a while and started walking. Had ½ sandwhich [sic] & piece of candy & cap of water in last 36 hr.

The escape maps show three trails heading north-

northwest from the desert; two starting about 175 miles southeast of Benghazi and one even farther southeast. One of them leads to Soluch and probably appears to correspond directly to the flight path they think they must have made into the desert. To their hopeful minds, this trail will be the one they are on, without doubt. The only question is where along the trail are they. There is only one way to find out.

They start walking in the rapidly spreading gloom. Light-blind from the glaring daytime sun, they require several minutes after sunset to adjust to the increasing darkness. At first a bright glaze seems continually in front of the eyes, but gradually it disappears and the stars become visible. The going is easier. The same northwest wind that had blown them so far into the desert springs up again, and for the first hour it feels good. Then the air grows just plain cold.

They rest methodically for ten or fifteen minutes every half hour or so, but keep walking steadily all through the early part of the night. Actually, it is not so bad as the night before, when they had tried to sleep in the cold. At least they keep warmer walking. The trail stands out plainly in the starlight and is not difficult to follow.

By midnight the men have covered what must be about ten more miles. They stop and make another marker. Then, physically exhausted, they roll up in their flight clothes and parachutes to try to sleep.

When daylight comes, six of them, inventorying

their belongings, discard their now useless Mae West preservers.

Huddle together for warmth in the early-morning cold. Dole out a candy square and a capful of the dwindling water to each. The surge of energy that comes from the tiny ration is remarkable. They feel so refreshed that they walk on until nearly noon. The group must now have covered about twenty-five miles from where they landed. Mildly heartened at the distance they are making, they establish a third marker and then erect shelters with the remaining parachute cloth, weight them down on the west-facing portion, and crawl underneath to ward off the rays of the merciless sun. Some tuck the loose edges of the shelters around their collars and hope their hats will keep the sun off their heads. That way they can doze without nodding and dropping their shelters.

There is no sound. No planes fly over, as hoped. The men squat dumbly and bake through the interminable afternoon.

Ripslinger writes in his diary:

Tuesday, April 6. Started out early walking & resting. It's not sundown and still going. One teaspoon of water today. The rest of the boys are doing fine.

As the men start their tramp in the growing darkness, no one has the courage to mention the fact that no planes had been seen. It is on each man's mind, obsessively, but speaking of it somehow seems as though it might bring bad luck. No, the thing to do is to keep hoping hard, and praying quietly. Maybe the planes will show tomorrow. Maybe they haven't worked this far south yet.

In the early evening the stumbling men come across a huge set of tracks, many feet wide, intersecting the trail they are following. For a few moments there is a surge of hope. The lines run north-northeast.

According to the maps they carry no tracks are supposed to be heading in that direction in this area. Everything heads north-northwest or plain northwest to Benghazi. Nothing runs northeast until reaching the Tobruk-Derna area which is far to the east. Close to Benghazi there are some paved roads that head northeast, but these new tracks are certainly no paved road. Maybe these are tracks made by Rommel's or Montgomery's armored forces last winter. And maybe not. They just might lead somewhere. And that somewhere could be close.

They must make a decision.

Two volunteers will head up the new track just in case. At two A.M., if you haven't found anything, turn back to the northwest and intercept us on this old trail. If you are close to anything, you should see some sign of it by two A.M. It doesn't seem likely, but we could somehow be in the Derna area. If so, you will know it by two A.M., judging the distance we've already walked. If nothing shows by then come back and join us. We'll stop at three and rest until after sunup. If you're not with us by then we'll stay put until nine A.M.

Hays and Adams decide to try the new trail. They start walking up the west side of the broad tracks at about 9 P.M.

The other six men make a fresh marker on the west side of the old trail, past the intersection, to show which way the main party has gone.

Later Hays and Adams are aware of an increasing doubt. Suppose, for some reason, they didn't again fetch up with the other party, as, for example, if they thought they saw a distant light at 2 A.M.? Maybe they had better leave a marker, just in case. So during a rest period they make a parachute-strip marker on the west side of the new trail pointing north-northeast. Adams drops his useless Mae West without noticing it. They walk on.

But, alone, the two are without the strength of conviction they had known when part of the group. They begin wondering how far it might be back to the old trail. Maybe it is farther than they think. Maybe at 2 A.M. they would be so far behind that they couldn't catch up with the other six. And the six had all of the water, what there was of it.

They change their course, carefully checking by flashlight and compass periodically to be sure they are headed right. By half stumbling, and half falling forward steadily, and sacrificing some of their rest periods, they intercept the old trail just at sunup. In another hour they have overtaken their comrades. Both men are utterly depleted.

None of the six needs to ask anything of Hays or Adams. The two will, understandably, be too tired to talk. Apparently they have found nothing, otherwise they wouldn't have come back. The two latecomers are given a share of the remaining rations, allowing them to wet their tongues with water, and the group establishes a sixth parachute marker (they had placed another along the old trail during the night).

The sore, dehydrating little party of wanderers lurches to its feet. By noon they have crept a few more agonizing miles up the trail. The sun is piercingly hot again by this time, so they fall into their customary routine of setting up their pitiful shelters. They may have made another fifteen miles since the evening before.

Before collapsing under his shelter, Toner writes up the preceding twenty-four hours:

Rested at 11:30, sun very warm, no breeze, spent P.M. *in hell, no planes, etc. rested until 5:00* P.M. *walked & rested all nite, 15 min. on, 5 off.*

The afternoon is further torment. The water in their bodies is evaporating rapidly. Lips are puffed and cracked, feet are pulsating lumps, so swollen that shoes can hardly be tied over them. Eyeballs are so dry that the men can hardly keep their slitted lids open. Blinking of eyelids has become excruciatingly painful over drying eyeball surfaces.

When the sun begins to cool in the west, Ripslinger writes in his diary:

Wednesday, April 7. Started early A.M. and walked til about near spent. Terrible hot afternoon. Started again at 6 P.M. and walked all night. One spoon full of water is all.

Again that night, after the miniscule rations are doled out, they plow dutifully, but ever more slowly, forward along the tracks. Rest periods are more frequent and longer. A final marker is made that night; then the parachute fabric is down to the bare minimum needed for each man's use. One of them drops an improvised face mask at the marker, probably without noticing the loss. Yet still they hobble, unspeaking, plodding through the sand, resting, getting up again, stumbling, resting, and back on their throbbing feet. It becomes harder and harder to get up. That night and the next morning they creep forward by sheer will, perhaps an additional fifteen miles, before it gets too hot to continue. When they stop at noon, there is so little parachute cloth left that they merely collapse on the sand and pull whatever shreds of parachute and clothing they have left over their exposed, scorching skin.

Faithfully, Toner notes the march in his diary:

Same routine, every one getting weak, can't get very far, prayers all the time, again P.M. very warm, hell. Can't sleep. Every one sore from ground.

That night, with only a whisper of rations and barely enough water to wet each man's tongue, they move again. Their unswerving discipline is remarkable. Many times during the night they stumble and fall to the sand. Those still upright help the fallen back to round-swollen feet so painful the ankles will hardly support them. If the night before has been hell, this night defies description for the weaker of them. Their bodies are one huge fevered, pulsing pain, and their lungs and throats seem half-filled with harsh sand dust. To talk is torture and requires too great an effort. Breathing and stumbling forward are about all they can accomplish.

Around midnight, the airmen come to the terrifying beginnings of the sand dunes. Gradually the sand grows deeper. They are too weak to admit such a staggering misfortune. They bravely ignore the shifting, sliding surfaces, and wade in, anyway. There is no track to follow now, so they rely on compasses. Again they endure a night of agony, of sliding, falling, pitching and groping. But this long, relentless torment, paced by the weaker men, produces only a pathetic ten miles more northwest.

Friday morning they must burrow as far as possible into the deepening sand for protection from the relentless sun. They shield their heads and faces as best they can with the scarce cloth and clothing left.

Toner, writing up the preceding twenty-four hours, records:

Hit Sand Dunes, very miserable, good wind but continuous blowing of sand, everybody now very weak, thought Sam & Moore were all gone. La Motte [sic] eyes are gone, everyone else's eyes are bad. Still going N.W.

And Ripslinger, later in the day, writes:

Friday, April 9. 5th day out & we all thought we're gone. All wanted to die during noon it was so hot. Morn & nite okay.

That night five of the men can go no farther. Hatton, Toner, Hays, Adams and LaMotte collapse. Not one of them can stand without help. Instead of the approximate 50 miles they calculate they have come, an incredible 65 miles have been covered. They can go no farther.

But Ripslinger, Moore and Shelley are still able to stand. Each of the three takes an escape compass and they trudge into the sand dunes together. They waver and stagger and slip, but they keep moving ahead. In a few minutes, all three are out of sight in the darkness.

The others, remaining where they have fallen, press deeper into the sand, trying to escape the cold.

Sometime Saturday, Toner fills the space in his diary marked Friday 9:

Shelley, Rip, Moore separate and try to go for help, rest of us all very weak, eyes bad. Not any travel, all want to die, still very little water. nites are about 35°, good N. wind, no shelter, 1 parachute left.

While the three grope northwest through the dunes at night and each morning, digging into the sand for protection during the hot part of the day, the other five men, too weak now even to get up, sit and watch the burning sun and heatless stars through slitted eyelids, hoping for signs of rescue. An accurate description of how they feel and of the shuddering, feverish anguish they endure is contained in the last three entries in Lieutenant Toner's diary:

SATURDAY, Apr. 10, 1943. Still having prayer meetings for help. No signs of anything, a couple of birds; good wind from N. Really weak now, can't walk, pains all over, still all want to die. Nites very cold, no sleep.

SUNDAY 11. Still waiting for help, still praying, eyes bad, lost all our wgt. aching all over, could make it if we had water; just enough left to put our tongue to, have hope for help very soon, no rest, still same place.

MONDAY 12. No help yet, very [unreadable] cold nite.

April 12th's entry is Lieutenant Toner's last. Perhaps he, or one of the other four, lives another day, but it is doubtful.

The five men of Toner's group not only have come 65 miles to the place where they die, they have lived at least eight day and nights with almost no water and on perhaps enough food for one or two days' requirements. It must also be remembered, in gauging their supreme endurance, that when these men had landed in the desert they had flown a grueling thirteen and a half hours and were physically and mentally exhausted to begin with.

After leaving the others, Ripslinger, Moore and Shelley trudge on northwest into the deepening dunes and treacherous, sinking, shifting drifts of the dreaded Sand Sea of Calanscio.

Late Saturday, as the three rest in the dunes, Ripslinger writes:

Saturday, April 10. Walked all day and night. Suggested Guy, Moore and I make out alone.

Ripslinger pushes more than twenty miles into the dunes before he, too, falls and dies. He keeps going at least through Sunday. On that date he writes his last diary entry:

Palm Sun. Still struggling to get out of dunes and find water.

Whether Moore pushes on after Ripslinger falls, it is impossible to say for his body has not been recovered as this is written, but, because Shelley's body was found, we know that he, drawing upon some extraordinary source of energy, staggers still another seven miles into the dunes before he can walk no more. He has trekked more than ninety miles since landing in the desert, the last two or three days with no water at all.

Sergeant Moore's body must lie beneath the sand dunes' shifting patterns somewhere in the vicinity of where Ripslinger's and Shelley's were found.

The dauntless courage and tenacity of these eight men in the face of danger, suffering, and unthought-of deprivation will remain a high point of human achievement against the most severe adversities. Since the beginning of time men have probably lain down and died when confronted with similar tests, sure that no human could possibly survive. The men of the *Lady Be Good* have given desert-survival schools a new gauge with which to indoctrinate their students, a measuring stick that may save other lives. And surely the needs of the eight men will inspire more adequate survival equipment.

The almost unbearably ironic twist to the story relates to one of the chief items designed to save them, their escape map.

They had faithfully carried the map with them until they fell. It was all they had. But it had been drawn only for escape from the northeast African coastal region; it ended approximately 70 miles north of where they fell.

If the map had continued another 120 miles south, and if the men had had the means of locating their position on it, they might have walked out of the plateau of death to El Gezira Oasis, only 130 miles away to the southwest.

From the bailout point to El Gezira their path would have led directly to the *Lady Be Good* and its radio, water and food. From the crashed bomber, the oasis was only 110 miles, of which only 35 miles were sand dunes.

Sergeant Shelley got through 27 miles of sand dunes with no water or food after having walked 5 days and 65 miles on less than 6 tablespoonfuls of water and very little food. And it was still 80 miles straight ahead for him to Gialo Oasis, of which 60 miles were dunes.

10

CAPTAIN OLDRICH DOLEZAL, of Benghazi, Libya, and Kent, England, is the Libyan equivalent of a Canadian bush pilot. A World War II Royal Air Force pilot, Dolezal now flies aircraft for the Silver City Airlines of Benghazi.

On February 11, 1960, Dolezal flew food, water and supplies to an oil exploration crew working in an area along the northwest edge of the plateau where the *Lady Be Good* had been found eleven months earlier.

The party was under contract to the British Petroleum Company, Ltd., successor to the 1959 D'Arcy Exploration Company. Leader of the contract party on the desert was an American, James W. Backhaus, of Burge, Wyoming. Backhaus was the adventurous type —like those who colonized the American West where he was born. His companions, too, came from faraway places in search of a well-paid challenge—the wresting of valuable oil from the valueless desert sands. The other men were Kenneth Moss, of London; Walter Hawk, of Alberta, Canada; and Gordon Brown, of Prince Edward Island, Canada. The men were investigating underground rock strata in a location they had dubbed "Failing Cap," about 56 miles north of Blockhouse Rock and about 75 miles north-northwest of the only other landmark on the plateau—the wreckage of the *Lady*.

Dolezal, like everyone else who got around in Libya, had heard in detail of the tremendous air-ground searches conducted by the Americans in 1959 in the attempt to locate bodies of the B-24's lost crew. For this reason, he was more than usually attentive to a message that Backhaus gave him when he landed to unload supplies on the desert plateau near Failing Cap.

When the hard-bitten, leather-faced desert pilot finished his unloading job, he thanked James Backhaus for the strange message, took off from the plateau, and immediately climbed for altitude. Reaching sufficient height, Dolezal fired up his radio and made a "long-distance" call to Idris Airport's radio control tower 710 miles away at Tripoli.

"Would you pass a message to the American Air Force people at Wheelus?" Dolezal asked Idris.

The tower would.

"Tell them that a party of men working in the dunes with British Petroleum have located some bodies which they think are aircrew of the old ghost bomber, *Lady Be Good*. The location of the bodies is twenty-six degrees fifty-four minutes north by twenty-four degrees eight minutes east. The ground party leader is named Backhaus. His party will be in the area for several days and will be easy to spot from the air. And, Tower—I am flying on into Idris. I am about seven hundred miles southeast at the moment."

When Wheelus Air Base received the surprising information from Idris Tower, the Air Force officers in Base Operations soon had every flat surface covered with maps. They identified the reported location by longitude and latitude and marked X's on their maps.

"It can't be!" one incredulous officer exclaimed. "That's in the exact area we searched most carefully last summer and fall!"

If the oil party had the co-ordinates right, the find was made just into the edge of the dunes, just off the northwest edge of the plateau, and a relatively short distance from the point where the old Italian vehicle tracks had disappeared into the sand.

Hurriedly, they made preparations for a verification flight to the plateau the next morning. By the time Dolezal landed at Idris, a call was waiting for him from Wheelus. It was an invitation to accompany the Americans to the desert.

Early on February 12th, Wheelus Base Commander Griffith cranked up a venerable old C-47 with extra fuel tanks, and the new desert party got under way for the long flight. Flying copilot for Griffith was Major Rubertus, the officer who had first landed at the *Lady Be Good* crash site. (Rubertus had barely arrived back from the States in time to make the flight. He had appeared in New York on February 2nd on the Armstrong television program about the *Lady* and its crew. Just ten days earlier that program had conjectured that the bodies of the nine men were probably lost in the sand dunes forever; precisely what the Army and Air Force had been convinced of since the preceding August.)

Also on this flight, was the chief of Wheelus Air Base chaplains, Lieutenant Colonel William G. Woods. This time it appeared as though his services would probably be needed.

The C-47 completed the lengthy flight to the plateau and had no trouble, with Dolezal's help, in locating the oil exploration party from the air. Backhaus' men set out smoke flares to indicate wind direction, and Griffith put his plane down with hardly a ripple.

Backhaus met the party with a couple of small trucks, and the group was immediately driven to the site of the oilmen's discovery.

Walt C. Wandell, a Wheelus information writer, described the scene as the men found it:

> Against a background of jumbled dunes and desert vastness, which gave the impression of a location on the moon, were the remnants of a pathetic little camp.
> Five bodies were closely grouped in an area littered

with canteens, flashlights, pieces of parachute fabric and harness, sheepskin-lined flight jackets, shoes, a Mae West [the eighth to be found on the plateau] life preserver and other readily identifiable bits of equipment and personal effects.

Oilmen joined the Wheelus party in a simple but impressive prayer ceremony over the remains.

After a hasty inspection of items of equipment, taking great care not to disturb anything that could help in positively identifying the bodies, Colonel Griffith directed that they be properly covered and kept at the location until experienced searchers got to the scene to conduct a thorough investigation. The colonel was satisfied that the men belonged to the *Lady Be Good* crew and that others of the crew might be buried nearby in the sand.

One of the items lying in the open left no doubt as to the identity of one of the bodies—a heat-curled sunglasses' case bearing the still clearly legible inscription 2ND LT. DP HAYS—navigator on the *Lady*'s last flight.

"It was apparent," Colonel Griffith said, "that the crew members had made temporary camp at a point where they probably had reached the limit of their endurance. This was after walking a minimum of fifty miles. It was quite evident that the group had maintained close discipline and had followed the prescribed desert-survival procedures to the very end."

On his return to Wheelus, Griffith contacted the

Army. The result was another hasty trip to the south for Captain Myron Fuller who had headed the unsuccessful search efforts the year before. With Fuller came Hugo A. Schaefer, an Army field investigator.

On February 17th, the search team was flown to the plateau by Colonel Benjamin S. Lambeth, Jr., the deputy base commander at Wheelus. This time the C-47 was equipped to stay in the desert until identification of the bodies was completed.

Carefully exploring the sand in the vicinity of the five bodies, the Army team discovered four sets of "dogtag" military identification pieces, a World War II Red Cross sweater, a canteen, a flight cap with a second lieutenant's bar pinned on it, a pair of leather gloves, a leather billfold containing an Egyptian banknote, a silk escape map of the North African coastal area, and several pairs of government-issue shoes which the men had apparently removed when their feet had become too swollen to walk.

After the Army's preliminary investigation, each of the incredibly well-preserved bodies of the five crewmen was draped with an American flag, and a second prayer service was said.

Captain Fuller had decided not to announce the identity of the men until the bodies could be flown to Frankfurt, Germany, where detailed comparisons of their teeth with World War II dental charts could be made, and where a thorough bone-structure study could be compared with the men's known physical characteristics.

Shortly after the recovery of the bodies, Fuller made a further discovery which caused him to change his mind about verifying the identity of the five men.

A perfectly preserved diary, the property of Lieutenant Robert Toner, was found in the sand.

At first Fuller refused to release the contents of the diary to the public. Normally, such personal effects are considered to be the inviolable property of the next of kin. Therefore, instead of making the exact wording of Toner's diary known, Fuller allowed a paraphrased statement to be made for the newspapers through Wheelus information office. The February 18, 1960, statement read:

> Entries in the diary indicate that only five of the nine members of the crew died at this location. One failed to join the party after bailout from the bomber, and three later left the group to continue on ahead for help.
>
> No positive personal identification has been made, but experts of the U. S. Army Mortuary Service were said to indicate the members of the group being recovered were 1st Lt. William J. Hatton, pilot; 2nd Lt. Robert F. Toner, co-pilot; 2nd Lt. Dp Hays, navigator; Tech. Sergeant Robert E. LaMotte, crew member; and Staff Sergeant Samuel R. Adams, crew member.
>
> The tentative identifications are indicated from diary entries, and from such physical evidence on the spot as

dog tags, an identity book, an Air Corps ring and other personal effects.

Capt. Myron C. Fuller, of Placerville, California, head of the mortuary team, said that the personal account found indicated that the man who failed to join the party after bailout was 2nd Lt. John S. Woravka, bombardier, and the three who left the main group were Tech. Sergeant Harold S. Ripslinger, Staff Sergeant Guy E. Shelley, and Staff Sergeant Vernon L. Moore.

These diary indications eliminated the possibility that other bodies would be found in this immediate location. It had been previously thought the remains of other members of the crew might be buried in the sand nearby.

Bailout time was established by the diary, which indicated that the five men in the group being recovered reached this location April 9th, five days after bailout. The last entry in the book was April 12th, but the exact date of death is unknown.

The public-information writer at Wheelus had done the best he could with the slim information he had been given.

To the millions of United States citizens who had followed the long-drawn-out story of the *Lady Be Good*'s crew, it was not sufficient for someone off in the Sahara Desert to tell them what Lieutenant Toner's diary had "indicated" to him. They wanted to read those words themselves and draw their own conclusions.

Another person's interpretation of what had occurred was, to many, a completely intolerable case of the military withholding information for no valid purpose.

Almost immediately, the Pentagon was assaulted by the news-wire services, by *Life* magazine, which happened to have members of its staff at Wheelus at that moment on a story on the *Lady Be Good,* by several national news services, and by the producer of the Armstrong Circle Theater—who had made a trip from New York to the Sahara in order to present the story accurately on television.

Under direction of the Pentagon, quick to react to genuine public sentiment, the wording of the diary was released at Wheelus Air Base on February 20th. But in a last effort—conceivably to spare relatives—the Army had censored two small phrases: "all want to die" and "still all want to die." The perhaps kindly intentioned censorship so incensed newsmen that the Pentagon was forced to send out orders a second time, directing that the diary's precise contents relating to the Naples raid and the crew's attempts to escape the desert be released immediately.

Life, just going to press at this time, was able to release the full wording of the diary in its issue of March 7, 1960. Superimposed above a two-page aerial photograph of the crashed *Lady Be Good* was a simple reproduction of the diary's four opened pages in Toner's handwriting.

Life commented, "If there had been any way out this

heroic effort would have saved them. There was none. The perverse fate which made them miss their air base held them to the end."

And still the story of the nine men and their bomber was not finished.

The Air Force and the Army decided to conduct a partnership search for the rest of the nine-man crew. It was felt that the last parachute marker found must have been placed on the British trail by Lieutenant Woravka, the "John" whom the other eight men never found, and that the three men who Toner said were separating from the main group to go for help would undoubtedly have continued northwest through the dunes. It seemed logical too that Woravka's body would be found in the Calanscio Sand Sea's dunes where the trail entered the shifting sand, and that the bodies of Ripslinger, Shelley and Moore would likewise be recovered in the Sand Sea, several miles farther than the point at which the first five had been discovered.

Another full-scale air-ground search was under way within a few days.

Again a C-130 Hercules was flown from Europe. It picked up two Army helicopters at Wheelus and flew them to the plateau via Benina Airport at Benghazi. The Army searchers set up a camp site for their helicopter search and hopefully called their part of the expedition "Operation Climax."

Meanwhile, two RF-101 jet reconnaissance fighters

were flown from Laon Air Base, France, and made photostrip maps of the entire area. When the helicopters began operations, the pilots had the detailed strip maps in hand to aid in marking off the exact territory as they searched it. The two-phase operation, begun late in March, was aided by Army personnel on the ground using vehicles which also had been flown to the desert by the big C-130.

But the massive search turned up nothing, and Operation Climax began to look fully as futile as the preceding summer's efforts. Worse, nothing new had been found, and except for the oil team's discovery, the searchers were right back where they'd been months before.

Just when it all seemed completely useless, word was received from the same British Petroleum Company team which had found the five bodies that two more of the *Lady Be Good*'s crewmen had been discovered far into the dunes past the end of the Italian tracks!

Hastening to the reported site of the new discovery, the weary military men found that one of the bodies was at 28 degrees and 10 minutes North latitude by 23 degrees and 5 minutes East longitude—an unbelievable 21 miles into the sand dunes from the point where the first five bodies had been found! This body was immediately identified as Sergeant Ripslinger, the flight engineer, from personal effects and a diary which he had kept through Sunday April 11, 1943.

The second body was 6 miles still farther into the dunes—27 miles from the place where Lieutenant Hatton and the other four men had died! It was that of Sergeant Shelley, a *Lady Be Good* waist gunner. Shelley had walked more than 90 miles in all since bailing out, and his last 27 miles through the dunes had been without a single drop of water—even though he had had only 5 canteen caps (not much more than a tablespoon per cap) in the 5 preceding days.

In Ripslinger's and Shelley's cases, the searchers found it difficult to believe that two men had made this unparalleled trek, with next to no water or food, through one of the most severe regions known, but they now saw complete proof of it. The two sergeants had continued ahead for help just as Toner's diary had said they would, but both had gone much farther than any of the searchers had anticipated.

The military searchers decided that the body of Sergeant Moore, the crewman who had started out with Ripslinger and Shelley, must be somewhere close to his two friends. They also supposed now that Woravka might be equally far into the sand dunes at the end of the British tracks. The assumption about Woravka was that he must have hesitated too long in leaving the plane when he parachuted, and as a consequence had dropped to earth too far away from the other eight to be able to catch up with them. However, he had evidently found their marked trail, followed it to the intersection of the two sets of vehicle tracks, disagreed with the track the others took, set off up the British track instead, and left a parachute marker of his own along the new route to show which way he had gone. While this theory appeared to tie together all of the seemingly unconnected clues, it was later proved to be wrong.

The bodies of Sergeant Ripslinger and Shelley were flown to Frankfurt, Germany, where they were positively identified.

The search by the desert crews continued, but the most exhaustive ground-and-air reconnaissance of suspected areas yielded no clue to the two men still missing. The searchers concluded that both had simply been buried in the sand and might never be found.

Again the military men returned to their bases and closed the case—leaving the barren plateau to the only people who had use for it: the exploration teams still searching for tell-tale signs of the existence of underground oil.

The Army made arrangements with the next of kin of each of the seven men recovered to bring the bodies home for final burial. The crewmen had waited seventeen years to be claimed from the desert. They were to be taken to their homes by military escorts and given long-delayed full military funerals if their relatives so desired.

One by one, seven of the *Lady Be Good*'s men came home. When the last of the seven was buried, the Army again reverently closed the books on the *Lady Be Good,* and referred the mass of reports incident to the case to its permanent files.

On August 11, 1960, however, Headquarters of the United States Air Forces in Europe, which had moved General Spicer and his 17th Air Force to Europe in the meantime, received another surprising message from Wheelus Air Base—by then the Weapons Training Center for the Air Force's European units. The message read:

> Discovery of human remains believed to be those of another crew member of the *Lady Be Good* U. S. ghost bomber which crashed in the Libyan Desert in 1943 was reported today.
>
> Word of the find was relayed to Wheelus through the U. S. Embassy at Benghazi by the British Petroleum Co.
>
> The location, 45 kilometers northwest of the company's oil well, "Janet," was given as 26 degrees 54 minutes North, and 24 degrees 8 minutes East.
>
> The report sent out from the desert oil-exploration area tentatively identified the remains as those of "a U. S. airman."
>
> It was similar discoveries in the area by employees of this company which led to recovery, first of five and and then of two additional bodies of the nine-member *Lady Be Good* crew.

This time, the Army authorized the Air Force to go

to the plateau and recover the remains without Army assistance.

Colonel Lambeth, and Major Rubertus, accompanied by Colonel Edward G. Cada, director of medical services at Wheelus, again flew a C-47 to the plateau. Their crew was fully equipped to spend whatever time was necessary in the desert.

Landing near the *Lady Be Good* wreckage, the men were met by a British Petroleum Company crew and taken to the body it had found. The body was clearly visible in the open desert about two miles north of the point where the Army had discontinued its initial circular search around the *Lady* in favor of following the Italian vehicle tracks to the north-northwest.

It lay on the plateau floor, completely dressed in a high-altitude flying suit, a Mae West life jacket, and a parachute harness. The parachute was still attached, and appeared to have opened only partially. It was amazing that the body and the parachute could have lain in plain sight of the searchers for a year without having been found—until it was remembered that the air-searches and ground sweeps had been made only on the northern part of the plateau and into the Sand Sea.

Doctor Cada immediately identified the body as that of Lieutenant John S. Woravka, the "John" referred to in Toner's diary. The search teams had concluded that he would be found in the Sand Sea past the end of the British tracks 65 miles to the north.

Ironically, a canteen three-quarters full of water—half again more than the other eight crew members had had among them—was found with Woravka's body. (When the contents of the canteen was sampled in a laboratory at Wheelus Air Base a few days later, the water was found to be free of bacteria or any other contamination after almost 17½ years.)

Colonel Lambeth and his party explored the area around Woravka's body on foot. Since no one had previously searched this section, they were reluctant to leave without a close examination. Their persistence was repaid.

A little more than a mile south the group came upon a large pile of bulky parachute harnesses from which the shroud lines and canopies had been cut. This was undoubtedly the spot where the other eight men of the *Lady Be Good* had assembled after bailout. Also, burned-out handles of signal flares were found in the vicinity, indicating that they had ignited the hand-held flares in an attempt to find Woravka when they missed him.

Colonel Lambeth flew Lieutenant Woravka's body back to Wheelus for transshipment to the Army at Frankfurt.

Only the body of Staff Sergeant Vernon L. Moore, waist gunner, was still to be found. Based upon the statement in Lieutenant Toner's diary that Moore, Ripslinger and Shelley had gone ahead together for help through the sand dunes to the northwest, it was a relative certainty that that was where his body might some day be discovered.

Since Woravka was found only 12 miles north-north-east of the *Lady Be Good* itself and had obviously been killed instantly upon impact with the desert floor, the earlier assumption that he had made the lone marker on the British tracks was invalid.

While no one now can explain how the lone marker came to be placed in its location, it is certain that Sergeant Moore did not place it there after he left the main party on April 10, 1943. To have done so, he would have had to backtrack more than 25 miles in the direction he had come from, and it is unlikely that a man barely able to move forward would have returned to where he knew there was nothing to help him.

The eighth marker must have had some other meaning, it was concluded. The diary found with Sergeant Ripslinger agreed with Lieutenant Toner's statements in almost every respect and made no mention of the eighth marker on the British trail. Oddly enough, neither diary mentioned any of the tracks the men had followed.

The Army asserted that there was nothing in the two small notebooks found with Woravka's body which would shed any light upon the *Lady Be Good* and her crew. The Army's word must be taken for this because neither of the notebooks was made public.

11

Scientifically there can be no such thing as a jinx. However, few scientists, given a choice, would not avoid an object long burdened with misfortune or disaster for those who have been closely associated with it.

The *Lady Be Good,* jinx or not, has left a distressing record behind her.

Beginning on April 4, 1943, at 7:50 P.M. over Sorrento, Italy, there were four crews flying together—with the *Lady Be Good* leading. Eight days later her crew was dead in the Sahara Desert of exposure and malnutrition.

Eighteen days after Lieutenant Hatton's men had died, misfortune struck the second of the four crews. On that day, Lieutenant Walter C. Swarner was killed in action.

A little more than two months passed before the third crew met an unknown fate. On July 4, 1943, Lieutenant Luther A. Worley and his crew were listed missing in action. They are still missing.

Of the four first pilots who flew that last ragged formation of Section B, 376th Bomb Group, on April 4, 1943, only Lieutenant Edwin L. Gluck survived the war. Gluck got out of the Air Corps and returned to civilian life as soon as the war ended. He now lives in a suburb of Pittsburgh and says he has only been up in an airplane twice in the last 16 years.

"I remember the mission all right," Gluck relates. "It was my fifth, and Hatton's was the first plane lost after I joined the Group. I remember it well.

"Hatton led us in from the diversionary course to Sardinia, and we made a landfall fairly close to where we were supposed to. It was probably an accident, if he was in the same boat as the rest of us. Anyway, I remember it was already too dark to bomb Naples at that time, so we turned around and headed back toward Soluch. I don't remember exactly where we broke formation, but it wasn't very far south because it got pitch dark in a hurry.

"After we broke up I had no confidence at all in my navigator. He had been suffering from anoxia for some time because of a leak in his oxygen mask. He didn't make good sense, even after we went down to lower altitude to bomb Catania airfield on the way back.

"After we unloaded the bombs we set some kind of

course for Soluch, but in an hour or so my engineer came up to the cockpit to tell me that we didn't have enough gas to get home. I immediately changed course for Malta, which was supposed to be closer—provided we were where we thought we were. Actually, it turned out that we had been nearer to Soluch than to Malta, and we just barely made it into the island. That's how good our navigation was in those days.

"We had no trouble landing on the short runway on Malta, except for burning through about three layers on each tire getting stopped. Just before I landed, Lieutenant Flavelle from Section A tried to get into the same airport, having been shot-up at Naples, and overshot the runway and ran through a ditch. He tore up the B-24, but I don't think anyone was seriously hurt as a result."

Gluck says that when he got back to Soluch the next day he heard about Hatton's not having returned from the raid, but everyone assumed that Hatton had run out of fuel—got lost on the way home—and had ditched the *Lady Be Good* in the sea.

"That's the last I ever heard about Hatton's crew until I saw the Armstrong Circle Theater on television," Gluck said. "It was quite a surprise after all these years to learn that he had gotten so far out in the desert."

Gluck survived all the known jinxes: He completed 35 bomber missions, was awarded the Distinguished

Flying Cross and "several" Air Medals, and returned to the United States without a scratch.

The original crew of the *Lady Be Good* was not nearly so lucky. Second Lieutenant Millard Kesler, the *Lady*'s first navigator, says:

"We began to have a pretty tough time after Lieutenant Hatton and our ship disappeared on April fourth. When we got back from Malta and found the *Lady Be Good* gone, we were stuck with that old spare ship for the rest of our tour.

"Our next mission was on April sixth, two days later. During that mission, our first time exposed to enemy fire, one of our gunners was killed by flak over the target. When we got back to Soluch we got permission to fly a Group plane over to the new field at Berca (which we were in the process of moving to) so we could bury our gunner there.

"After that, it looked like we might have broken our jinx," Kesler continued. "We were still flying the spare ship, of course, and she was so old that there were fixed machine guns on her nose—like a World War I Spad. We got all the way to July thirteenth in Forty-three in that old ship before the boom was lowered on us again.

"On that date we had a rough mission, and three of our gunners were wounded, and the plane was shot up pretty bad. All three gunners had to be hospitalized, but the old clunker was fixed up just in time for us to make a July fifteenth mission with three replacement gunners.

"By then all our crew except Lieutenant Rose, our pilot, had had twenty-seven combat missions and two hundred and twenty-seven combat hours each. Rose had one more mission than the rest of us because he'd volunteered to fly an extra mission in honor of his mother on Mother's Day. We were so close to going home with our required thirty missions that we were all beginning to get the shakes just thinking about it.

"The July fifteenth mission was to Bari, Italy. I don't think any of the crew is likely to forget that one. We were hit by flak over the target, and the old ship just practically blew right out from under us.

"How we did it, I don't know, but all of us managed to parachute successfully. As we floated down we could see a mob of Italian soldiers with guns waiting for us— a welcoming committee. There wasn't any sense in resisting under those circumstances. We were captured and put in the Bari city jail. I remember thinking how lucky our three gunners were to be in the hospital. They would be out before long, fly three more missions, and go home.

"Our crew was kept together through several Italian prisons; then to Moosburg, Germany; then Stalag Luft III at Sagan in East Germany. We stayed there until February of Forty-five when the advancing Russians forced the Germans to move us back to Moosburg.

"Imagine our surprise, when in April we were reunited in Moosburg with our three 'lucky' gunners. The poor devils had gotten out of the hospital back in Libya with only three missions to go, and had been shot down with another crew and captured not long after the rest of us. Brother, that *Lady Be Good* luck stayed right with us."

Kesler also said that after his crew was finally liberated, they all returned to the United States where most of them were discharged from the Air Force. "All of us still held the same rank—after all that—which we had held when we got to Soluch two and a half years earlier. Not one single promotion for the lot of us."

Kesler has been on and off active duty as a reserve officer in commissioned grades up through captain. Currently, he is back on active duty as a staff sergeant—having decided to put in twenty years so that he will be eligible to retire from the Air Force. He is stationed at Wright-Patterson Air Force Base, Dayton, Ohio, where he runs the Book Department Store for the Air Force Institute of Technology.

Lieutenant Rose is still a civilian—although Kesler says he has some military-reserve affiliation. Rose lives on a farm near Ivanhoe, California.

On the whole the 376th had had good luck before April 1943 when the *Lady Be Good* came to join its bomber fleet. Its record, made under the worst operating conditions possible and flown largely without any kind of fighter escort, had been exemplary. But that

luck grew worse beginning in the late spring of 1943—
first with individual losses and finally with misfortunes
which involved the entire Group.

During the early summer of 1943 rumors began to
drift among the 376th's crews about an impending raid
that would be the real thing. And they proved true.

Some very strange target patterns were laid out in
the surrounding desert and all the crews began practic-
ing low-level runs on them in between combat missions.

Besides Compton's 376th Group and "Killer" Kane's
98th Group of B-24s (comprising the whole U. S. Ninth
Air Force Bomber Command's heavy fleet), three more
B-24 groups were imported to Benghazi from England
for this one special mission. The imported groups were
the 93rd, the 44th and the 389th.

The air traffic around Benghazi became as busy as
that around Washington National, LaGuardia, and
Chicago O'Hare airports combined. This *was* going to
be a big one!

When the word was finally given to the participating
crews—just before the raid—everyone was stunned. The
big mission was to be a low-level attack by high-altitude
heavy bombers against the vital Axis oil refineries at
Ploesti, Romania, 1,100 miles away. Practice targets in
the desert had been laid out to geographically simulate
the oil refineries! Altitude en route to the target was
to be at treetop level in order to catch enemy radars,
antiaircraft guns and fighter planes by surprise. (Reconnaissance flights had spotted a considerable build-up

in enemy air strength and antiaircraft emplacements since the initial high-level raid by B-24s back in June 1942.)

The 376th was to lead the raid, and for that purpose a select crew had been chosen for intensive briefing and training for pinpoint navigation while flying right next to the ground. Compton, who never missed a dangerous mission, was to fly in the 376th formation with Brigadier General Ent, chief of the Ninth Bomber Command, aboard his plane.

Early in the morning of August 1, 1943, the specially trained 376th Group lead crew took off from Berca. By 7:40 there were 175 B-24s off the ground to follow him. But shortly after take-off the lead plane plunged into the Mediterranean and its crew was killed.

Keith Compton, whose men say he never backed down from a challenge, moved up through the formation and took over the lead. Even though his crew had no more training than the rest, Compton felt that, as Group Commander, he should now assume this responsibility. It was *his* crew, his specially trained lead crew, that had crashed, so the mission leadership still fell to the 376th.

En route to Yugoslavia, which was on the path to the Romanian targets, another B-24 crashed in the sea, and eleven more aborted because of various mechanical troubles. The bomber force reached Yugoslavia with 163—13 big B-24s less than at take-off.

Flying over the Yugoslav mountains en route to

Romania, the five Groups encountered extensive cumulus clouds, after which they had considerable trouble getting back in formation. In the confusion, only Compton's 376th and Lieutenant Colonel Addison Baker's 93rd Group headed forward on schedule over the first checkpoint at Pitesti. The 44th and 389th Groups got back together all right, but they circled, waiting for Kane's 98th to appear, and lost twenty minutes. Meanwhile, Compton and Baker's Groups were still charging ahead at treetop level—twenty minutes out in front of the other three Groups.

All of this was bad enough, but when Compton and Ent roared over the rooftops of Târgoviște, the crew mistook the town for Floreshty—the initial point where a sharp right turn was to be taken for the run-in on the Ploesti oil fields. So the 376th led the 93rd in a right turn 50 miles too early and headed directly southeast for Bucharest, the capital city of Romania.

The mistake is more readily understood when it is considered that navigating a heavy bomber in hostile territory at 200 miles an hour over the rooftops—without the specially prepared charts and precise practice which had crashed with the lead crew—is similar to trying to drive a car 100 miles an hour without ever missing or misreading a highway sign or making a wrong turn, even though you've never driven the route before.

This grave error was multiplied by the fact that the other three Groups were 20 minutes back and did not

know that the first two had made a wrong turn. Had
they all stayed together, the mistake might not have
been too serious—as a matter of fact it might have lent
even further confusion to enemy defenses. Unfortunately for everyone, however, the last three Groups
navigated correctly for the target and were making up
all the 20 minutes lost time, and more.

Speeding to the southeast, no one in Compton's crew
was able to recognize the precise error that had been
made until the two Groups went bursting into the
suburbs of Bucharest. Recognizing then where they
were, Compton, followed by Baker, made a sharp left
turn to the north to return to Ploesti and attack the oil
fields from the south. By this time there were B-24s
swarming all over central Romania at treetop height,
and enemy defenses were thoroughly alerted. Compton
and Ent realized the danger of attacking the targets
regardless of their error, but more than this was needed
to turn these dedicated crews from so important a target
—especially when they had almost reached it.

As luck would have it, just as Compton's B-24s ap-
proached the oil fields from the south, the other three
Groups were beginning their attacks from the northwest. To have continued his course to the north would
have put Compton and Baker's B-24s in the position of
flying almost head-on, at almost zero altitude, through
the other three Groups. Making the best of a bad break,
Compton lead his Group slightly east, then north, in-
tending to attack his targets after the other three

Groups, and from the same direction in which they were flying.

But when Compton turned east, Baker continued straight in. Baker's B-24 was blown up over the target, but he bombed successfully anyway, as did many of the crews following him. By this time, B-24s were pouring in over the oil fields from every direction, and falling in flames.

General Ent broke radio silence (which by then had become useless) and gave the 376th Group's pilots permission to attack "targets of opportunity" rather than allow the bombers to try to hold formation through the chaos. From that point on, it was every man for himself.

Only the 389th Group, which had a somewhat remote special target at Campina, was able to hit properly and get away with minimum losses. The rest bombed as best they could through the fire and smoke of burning, exploding oil refineries and B-24s.

As the battered bombers left the target area, they still had 1,100 miles to go to get home. German and Romanian fighters pounced, raining cannon and machine-gun fire on them for the first several hundred miles of the way back.

On this one raid, in which the 376th Group's slipping luck had figured so prominently, 41 B-24s were lost over the target, another 13 were shot down or crashed on the way home, 440 airmen were either killed or listed as missing in action, and another 100 flyers were either captured or interned in neutral Turkey—to which they had flown their crippled planes rather than crash them in the Mediterranean.

It was the most disastrous single raid by American aircraft during the whole of World War II. Five Medals of Honor, the nation's highest award, went to: Lieutenant Colonel Addison Baker, Commander of the 93rd (posthumously) and his copilot, Major John L. Jerstad; Colonel Leon W. Johnson, Commander of the 44th; Colonel John R. Kane, Commander of the 98th; and (posthumously) a lone pilot of the 389th, Lieutenant Lloyd H. Hughes, who attacked his Campina target successfully although his plane was already hit and trailing 100 octane fuel when he attacked—and exploded with his target.

Colonel Compton was awarded the Distinguished Service Cross, the second highest decoration. His 376th Group crews had shown tight discipline and tenacious courage in attacking their targets, even in the face of one of the worst breaks in the whole war.

Jack Preble, former Intelligence officer for the 376th's 515th Squadron, who had also been in World War I, said of Compton's part in the Ploesti raid:

"Keith was sure due a lot of credit for taking over the lead position after his select crew was killed. The kind of man he was, though, Keith wouldn't have shunted off that responsibility on anyone else. And I'll tell you another thing: Even after that raid we had the best *esprit de corps* of any bomber outfit in the Air

Corps. Our crews would follow Keith anywhere, any time. He was a great leader."

The luck of the 376th continued to tumble. If there was any possibility of things going wrong for it—things went wrong.

The Group's worst disaster is best told in the words of a man who survived it because he wasn't there. This was Lieutenant Myron T. Holmes, a bombardier with the 512th Squadron, who recalls that:

"On the twenty-eighth of December in Forty-three, the Group made a raid at Udine, up in Northern Italy. We had raided this area so many times that everyone called it a milk run. At the time, my crew was on rest leave on the island of Capri—which is why I'm here to tell you about it.

"While en route to the target that day, without escort, the Group was bounced by Goering's "Yellownose Circus" which was the Luftwaffe's cream of the crop. The Yellownoses concentrated first on my squadron and kept at them until they shot down every single B-Twenty-four in the whole squadron. Then they started working up through the rest of the Group and got quite a few more before the Group could get out of the fighters' range.

"When I returned from Capri to San Pancrazio Salentino, where we were stationed, my crew was the only crew left in the Five Hundred and Twelfth. It gave one a somewhat wierd feeling to return to his people, observe the flapping of the tents, and know that all his buddies were gone."

But even after this almost unacceptable damage, the 376th re-outfitted and went right along with the war—its morale badly shaken, but far from broken.

Lieutenant Paul Fallon, who had flown from the United States in the same formation with Hatton, was one of the survivors. Fallon was lucky. He says:

"I managed to fly forty-nine missions with the Three Hundred and Seventy-sixth. On my very last one I was shot down over Athens. But my parachute opened okay, and the Greek underground picked me up before the Germans could get me."

With the aid of underground workers, Fallon escaped to American forces. He was awarded the Air Medal with seven Oak Leaf Clusters and also the Purple Heart for a wound received during a bombing raid. Still in the Air Force, he is now a lieutenant colonel and is stationed at Eglin Air Force Base, Florida, with the Air Force Systems Command.

Another former lieutenant who survived the war is the man who signed off the *Lady Be Good*'s Maintenance Inspection Record before her last flight—Norman C. Appold. Appold is now a full colonel with the Air Force Satellite Systems Division at Inglewood, California. He and Fallon both appeared on the television series about the *Lady Be Good*.

"Old Retread" Jack Preble helped another former

member, Wiley L. Golden, of Cincinnati, to form the "376th Heavy Bombardment Group National Association" following the war. More than 500 ex-Group members attended the first reunion in Cincinnati, and the association met annually for several years. Prebble is retired and lives in Steubenville, Ohio.

Martin R. Walsh, the "old-timer" who broke formation and went alone to bomb the alternate target at Crotone on that April 4th, flew 37 missions before returning to the United States. He received the Distinguished Flying Cross, the Air Medal with two Oak Leaf Clusters and the Purple Heart. He is still on active duty with the Air Force as a Regular lieutenant colonel.

Myron T. Holmes, one of the lone survivors of the 512th Squadron of the 376th, is today an Air Force captain on active duty with the Strategic Air Command. He is stationed at Plattsburg Air Force Base, New York, where he is Director of Administrative Services for the 380th Bomb Wing (B-47).

Holmes made, in all, 38 raids with the 376th over Italy, Greece, Rhodes, Austria, Germany, France and Romania. His crew, which undoubtedly felt lucky in being the sole survivors of the 512th Squadron at one time, and after successfully getting through disastrous raids on Regensburg, Germany, and Steyr, Austria, eventually ran into trouble like so many others in the 376th.

"We had three crash landings after returning from missions," Holmes said, "and it seemed like we had survived almost everything. But my pilot, Fritz Sandburg, was killed on a training flight once we got back to the States, and my copilot, Rudolph Wilderman, was permanently disabled in a B-Twenty-four crash which occurred while he was ferrying the plane from Italy to England."

Keith Compton went back to the U. S. after the 376th moved to Italy. Today he wears a major general's stars and is at present Director of Operations for Strategic Air Command's bomber and missile forces.

It would seem reasonable to hope that once the war was over, and the wartime 376th Bomb Group disbanded, the string of misfortune which appeared to surround all those associated with the *Lady Be Good* would have ended. But it was not so.

The *Lady's* influence seemed to come to an evil climax while the searches in the desert for her crew were still going on.

When Major Rubertus flew the first search crew to land at the site of the *Lady's* crash in May, 1959, the old SC-47 he flew provided what seemed then to be an interesting, harmless side story. As stated, the *Lady's* undamaged radio set was removed and installed in the SC-47 to replace one that had gone out of commission, and had worked perfectly, to everyone's surprise. It was still installed in the SC-47 when, in June, 1959, the plane—flown by Captain Guy M. Allphin of Arlington, Kansas—ran into a violent *ghibli* sandstorm which forced him to ditch it in the Mediterranean. Impact with the heavy seas ripped off a propeller which hurtled into the cockpit and killed Captain Allphin.

An Army L-19 Otter aircraft, used by the Engineer Geodetic detachment at Benina Airport, Benghazi, where the U. S. Army was conducting geodetic surveys for the Libyan Government, was one of the first to be flown to the desert plateau where the *Lady* crashed.

While in the desert, the Otter's crewmen noticed that the pilots' armrests in the *Lady* were better designed than those in the Otter. They "salvaged" them and later mounted them in their own plane. The armrests proved so comfortable that they had others designed like them which they installed in the Otter for their passengers. The Otter was frequently used as a courier plane to fly from Benghazi to Tripoli and back.

In January, 1960, while making one of these runs with ten men aboard, the Otter ran into a *ghibli* and was never seen again. No one ever found out what happened and the ten persons were never found, but a few pieces of wreckage floated to land. Among them were pieces of the *Lady*'s armrests.

The list is long—and has grown longer through the years—of those who have reason to wish the *Lady Be Good* had never been built.

Yet in her deadly way the *Lady Be Good* and the unfortunate men who last flew her may have contributed to the advancement of survival expertise and techniques, and to the art of preserving hydraulic mechanical parts to a degree that may prove of vital importance.

12

THE MEN OF THE British Petroleum Company who found the *Lady Be Good* and her eight crewmen continue to explore the Cyrenaican Desert for oil. Mr. T. Bickford, area superintendent for the company, says that his Libyan operation has had just under 1,000 people working in several survey teams in different parts of the desolate country.

"During the past two years, when our effort reached its peak," Bickford said, "we have had in the field seven geophysical parties, four geological parties, two top-ographical-survey parties, four deep-test oil rigs and several water-well rigs. We have discovered oil in small quantities in Tripolitania, but not yet in Cyrenaica. We are currently drilling to the north and west of the Calanscio Sand [his word] Sea some one hundred to a hundred and fifty miles from where the bomber was found, and it is expected that this may prove to be our most productive area."

Bickford says that 75 per cent of his working crews are natives of Libya—the people who so desperately need economic help. And if oil is discovered in quantity in the area perhaps the reputed curse of the dread desert region will be lifted as local workmen pour into it, as producing wells are brought in, as pipelines are laid, and as the economic solution the country so sorely needs is found beneath this once totally uninhabited region.

Perhaps someday, when the capricious desert winds have shifted the endlessly moving sands at the right place, these men—or those who come after them—may find the body of Staff Sergeant Vernon L. Moore.

The *Lady Be Good* herself still lies abandoned on the bleak plateau in Cyrenaica and will probably remain there forever. But many parts of her have been taken away—for a clear purpose.

Hydraulic actuators of her landing gear and landing-flap system, and of her tail-gun turret-drive mechanism —along with a gun charger, hydraulic pumps, pressure accumulators and samples of the hydraulic fluid in her line—were removed and taken to Wright-Patterson Air Force Base at Dayton, Ohio, for examination by the Air Force's Aeronautical Systems Division.

This division contracted with the Vickers Company of Detroit and the Petroleum Refining Laboratory of

Pennsylvania State University, respectively, to analyze
the parts and the hydraulic fluid. Such studies might
uncover new techniques for the long-term storage of
similar materiel used in Air Force ballistic missiles—
which must now be stored in "inverted silos" deep in
the ground, on ready-firing alert, for many months at a
time.

Pennsylvania State University's report on a laboratory analysis of the *Lady*'s hydraulic fluid showed that
its wear and lubrication properties compared most
favorably with freshly prepared fluids of similar com-
position; that its initial oxidation and corrosion specifications had been unusually well maintained; and
that it showed excellent stability after the severe storage
conditions of the North African desert.

The same sort of exceptional preservation was true—
even with extreme temperature variations every day
and night for more than 16 years—in the case of every
part of the *Lady* which was subjected to test. Her radio-
compass set was still operative (her command radio and
VHF set were damaged in the crash and could not be
tested similarly). Further, the Vickers Company found
the parts it tested to have intact pressure seals, still soft
lubricants and no rust at all.

An obvious conclusion is that any aircraft or missile
system which can be kept in an atmospheric environment similar to that of the Libyan Desert can be ready
for immediate use even after prolonged storage. In the
case of intercontinental ballistic missiles of the 1960's,

this knowledge could well be of tremendous significance to the United States.

The *Lady Be Good* has also been memorialized.

One of her propellers, along with photographs of the bomber as she was found in the desert, is on permanent display at the Air Force Museum at Wright-Patterson Air Force Base.

Major Robert L. Bryant, Jr., director of the museum, says that Major General Spicer (who was based at Tripoli when the *Lady* was first located) is sending the museum one of the *Lady*'s .50 caliber machine guns to be included in the display. Also that a relative of one of the crewmen is sending him a canteen found with the bodies in the desert. This, too, will be displayed.

At Wheelus Air Base, Tripoli, a second of the *Lady*'s propellers is mounted at the foot of the main base flagpole, with a commemorative plaque beneath it.

In the main chapel at Wheelus there is a fitting memorial to Lieutenant Hatton's crew and to the *Lady Be Good*. Air Force men at the base, working with the chaplain, commissioned West German artist Peter Hess to create a stained-glass memorial window. The lead-mullioned panes are in a frame 17½ feet tall, and their rich, deep colors are in the finest tradition of European craftsmanship.

The window pictures a crashed and broken B-24 lying on the desert floor while three supersonic F-100 Supersabre jet fighters scorch across the sky overhead in close formation. (The F-100s symbolize the mission of Wheelus today: That of serving as the weapons-training center for all the United States Air Forces in Europe.)

An eternal flame burns on a memorial shaft under the window. Below the shaft are the words:

IN MEMORY OF NINE WHO MADE THE DESERT A HIGHWAY FOR OUR GOD. ANNO DOMINI 1943. LORD GUARD AND GUIDE THE MEN WHO FLY.

EPILOGUE

EPILOGUE

In the intervening years since 1961 when this book was written, many additional facts have come to light. International events which have taken place have also had a direct impact on the tragic story of the Lady Be Good and her ill-fated crew.

One of the first reports from pilots who inspected the bomber's cockpit initially puzzled Pentagon officers who were following the story. The pilots said that the throttles on the Lady's number one, two and three engines were found in full-off position, that all three of those engines' propellers were set for feathering, that all three of those engines' fuel-mixture controls and their master ignition switches were turned off. The pilots said that the automatic pilot also was turned to "off" position. The controls for number four engine, however, had been set for full-throttle operation. This last engine was the one running at full-blast when the Lady settled to the desert floor. Why would Hatton and Toner have set up the bomber in this configuration before parachuting? And why would they not have the automatic pilot turned on to steady the big ship while they jumped?

The most likely answers to those questions were that as the engines began running out of fuel, with only number four showing enough fuel to run for a few minutes, the aircraft would have veered sharply to the left if the propellers to the three dead engines had been left windmilling like huge air brakes. The right outboard engine running at full throttle would further have increased the left-veer tendency. It would have made better sense to feather the dead engines' propellers quickly so that they would streamline into the on-coming air and quit rotating. Then the airplane could be rapidly trimmed so that it could fly as nearly level as possible on number four engine while the last crewmen, Toner, and then Hatton, parachuted.

That the pilots were successful in nearly getting the bomber to fly level, hands-off, without engaging the unreliable auto-pilot is evident by the almost flat angle at which it struck the desert. Had either wing been low, it would have struck first, the wing would have broken off, and the bomber would most likely have cartwheeled. If the nose had been down at much of an angle, the bomber would probably have crumpled and the tanks feeding the number four engine likely would have ruptured and exploded.

As can be seen by examining the photographs of the wreckage, the Lady Be Good must have struck the hard sand floor nearly level—allowing the strongly turning propeller of number four engine to plow its way through the sand and break off from the crankshaft. The wings were not broken off or ruptured, and whatever fuel remained simply settled into the tank and eventually evaporated.

The other three propellers are more difficult to account for. Numbers one and three appear to have been wind-milling at least at a fairly slow rpm—regardless of having been set to feather—since all three blades on each propeller show the characteristic curling of a rotating propeller which has struck the ground. Number two's blades also show the characteristic curling, but to a much lesser extent, which indicates that the blades were nearly feathered but still rotating slowly.

None of the preceding suppositions really added to or les-

Central display board in Air Force Museum exhibit memorializing the Lady Be Good and her crew. The nosewheel tire (lower center) is still inflated. Rib at upper center is from a Lady Be Good aileron. Various items of mechanical equipment at right center were removed for testing and found to be in working order. Photos are of the Lady's crew, B-24s on a flight line in North Africa and scenes taken during the desert search. A closeup of personal equipment items (left) and crew-filled forms follows.

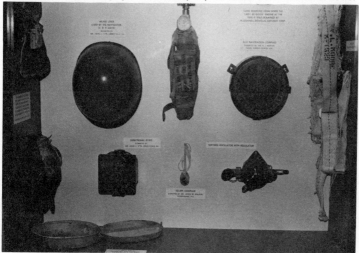

These items were for the most part acquired by relatives of the Lady's crew and donated to the Air Force Museum. Shown are Lt. Dp Hays' helmet liner, the cut-away parachute harness of Staff Sergeant Vernon L. Moore, a directional gyro, an escape compass, a D-12 navigational compass, a canteen of the crew's and a mess kit. At top right is a plastic container of fine sand taken from inside the Lady's number two engine by McDonnell-Douglas technicians.

sened the basic premises of the book and the story of the
Lady's last flight until an event which occurred in 1968. In
that year the British still operated a Royal Air Force Base
at El Adem, near Tobruk. Tobruk was much closer—380
miles—to the Lady Be Good wreckage than was Wheelus
Air Base. In 1968, unable to get the U.S. Air Force to make
yet another flight to the wreckage from Wheelus to get parts
he wished to have analyzed for sand and climate damage,
James W. Walker, then with the prominent aerospace firm
of McDonnell-Douglas, prevailed upon the Royal Air
Force. He talked the commander of the RAF Desert Rescue
School at El Adem into taking his training class and vehicles to the bomber's wreckage to obtain parts for analysis—
especially including engine cylinder heads. Glad of an opportunity for a real desert navigation and survival exercise
instead of an artificial one, the RAF commander obliged.

The RAF team reached the Lady Be Good in April 1968,
the same month in which Hatton had tried to lead his crew
out of the desert 25 years earlier. The RAF team reported
130 degree temperature and said that the unbearable heat
made it impossible to labor very long at removing individual
parts. Instead, they removed the entire number two
engine—cowling and all—from the Lady's left wing and got
it aboard one of their trucks. When the engine reached El
Adem, Walker arranged to have it flown to St. Louis for examination.

The McDonnell-Douglas examination revealed a fragment of a 20 millimeter cannon projectile lodge in the
rocker box cover atop the number one cylinder of the
engine.

A cannon projectile of that caliber could only have come

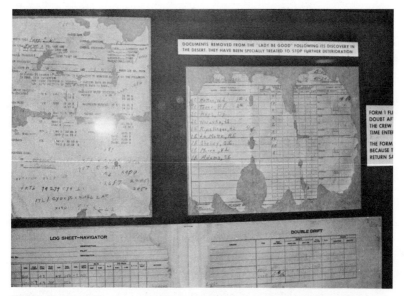

DOCUMENTS REMOVED FROM THE "LADY BE GOOD" FOLLOWING ITS DISCOVERY IN
THE DESERT. THEY HAVE BEEN SPECIALLY TREATED TO STOP FURTHER DETERIORATION

LOG SHEET—NAVIGATOR

DOUBLE DRIFT

The radio log and notes of Technical Sergeant Robert E. LaMotte, the Lady's
radio operator, and the incomplete Form 1A noting only members of the crew
and crew positions. Takeoff time is noted at 1450 (2:50 p.m.) local time.

The Lady's number two engine and cowling as displayed in the Air Force
Museum.

from an enemy fighter, considering the altitude the bomber was flying just before dark, and it must have come from a head-on pass since there was not a single bullet or flak hole anywhere in the fuselage, wings, cowling or tail surfaces of the Lady. The cannon shell must have entered the open cowling on the front of the air-cooled engine, ricocheted from a sturdy steel component and lodged in the relatively fragile rocker box cover.

The attack must have occurred just at dark, and after the other three bombers in the final formation had separated over Cape Licosa, Italy. None of the other three crews reported an enemy air attack. It must have also been too dark for the enemy pilot to find the Lady Be Good again if he circled to make another attack. It was that same darkness that all the other 376th Bomb Group pilots had counted on to hide them safely from air attacks while they found their ways home singly instead of in formation. A formation would have been decidedly easier to locate in the dark with either ground or airborne radar.

It is probable that Hatton and Toner feathered number two propeller and shut down its engine after the damage, flying on to Africa on three engines. It also seems likely that even though flying with only three engines, Hatton must have tried to find an alternate target on which to drop his bombs—as others had—because he held onto his heavy load of bombs until 10 p.m. according to Ripslinger's diary. At this time, Hatton apparently dropped the bombs in the open sea to avoid unnecessary strain on the remaining engines.

The enemy fighter attack has one major bearing on the basic story: Such a frightening experience, flying all alone after dark, not knowing for sure if another attack was coming, must have caused considerable additional tension among the inexperienced crew trying so hard to get their big bomber back safely to Soluch. That extra tension could well have further contributed to errors in judgement. It is strange that neither of the crews' diaries mentioned the enemy fighter attack unless we consider that the crew faced a much more absorbing problem at the time the diary notes were written.

Besides the discovery of attack damage to the Lady Be Good, the McDonnell-Douglas analysis of number two engine found a considerable amount of fine sand inside the engine. This fact, more than any theory, must explain why so many of Section B's crews reported serious mechanical

"LADY BE GOOD" ENGINE

The No. 2 (left inboard) engine retrieved for the Air Force Museum from the crash site in April 1968 by the RAF Desert Rescue Team based at El Adem, Libya. Upon examination at McDonnell-Douglas Aircraft Corp. in St. Louis, Mo., a piece of a 20mm projectile was found inside the rocker-box cover on the No. 1 cylinder, indicating that sometime during its mission, the "Lady Be Good" had been attacked in the air by at least one enemy fighter plane.

The engine still contains much of the sand found on it at the time it was removed from the desert. Most of the tan-color camouflage paint which was on the cowl in 1943 was worn off by blowing sand during the 25 years in the desert, leaving the original olive drab.

THE FRAGMENT OF THE 20 mm PROJECTILE
WHICH WAS FOUND INSIDE THE ROCKER-BOX
COVER OF THE NO. 1 CYLINDER OF THE NO. 2
"LADY BE GOOD" ENGINE UPON ITS TECHNICAL
EXAMINATION AT McDONNELL-DOUGLAS
AIRCRAFT CORP.

Closeup of the Lady's number two engine with small display of 20 millimeter cannon projectile fragment found by McDonnell-Douglas technicians in number one cylinder rocker box cover.

troubles after takeoff which forced them to abort the mission early and return to Soluch.

The year after the RAF and Walker retrieved the engine from the Lady Be Good, King Idris of the United Kingdom of Libya was on a visit to Turkey when a young Libyan Army corporal, Muammar Kaddafy, led a military coup which overthrew the monarchy. A devout Moslem fundamentalist and radical, Khadafy has been one of the Arab leaders who allied his government with the Soviet Union and vows, with others, "to push the usurping Israelis into the sea." He has no love for the United States and the United Kingdom because of their military and economic aid to Israel. Among his first demands were for the Americans to evacuate their Wheelus Air Base at Tripoli and for the British to evacuate El Adem RAF Base at Tobruk.

The major impact of the closure of Wheelus Air Base upon the Lady Be Good story was that the Air Force Museum at Wright-Patterson Air Force Base, Dayton, Ohio, received much of the memorial tributes to the Lady's crew which had been established at Wheelus.

Already the Museum had accumulated considerable Lady Be Good memorabilia—one of her .50 caliber machine guns, items of personal equipment of the crew donated by relatives, hydraulic and mechanical control actuators, the bomber's nose wheel and tire and many on-scene photographs. McDonnell-Douglas had contributed the number two engine and cowling, along with the cannon projectile fragment and a vial containing fine sand taken from inside the engine. From Wheelus Air Base came the Lady Be Good propeller which had been mounted on a pedestal outside the Base Chapel, and the magnificent large stained glass memorial to the crewmen which had been fashioned in West Germany at Besigheim, Baden-Wurttemberg, by artist and craftsman Peter Hess. The lead-mullioned paneled window was taken apart piece by piece and reassembled as the centerpiece of an exhibit in the Air Force Museum depicting the work of Air Force chaplains. When this impressive display was completed it was formally dedicated by Maj. Gen. Roy M. Terry, Chief of Air Force chaplains.

About the other three Lady Be Good propellers: One was acquired by the British Petroleum Company whose oil exploration parties had discovered the Lady Be Good and all of its crewmen who have been found. Another is enshrined at the U.S. Air Force Academy, and the last was made into a monument at Lake Linden, Michigan, the boyhood home of Technical Sergeant Robert E. LaMotte, the Lady's radio operator.

The U.S. Army Quartermaster Museum at Fort Lee, Virginia, also has a display of government-issue watches of the crewmen, items of clothing and some of their survival equipment.

The story of the Lady Be Good and its unfortunate crew will not be complete until the remains of Staff Sergeant Vernon L. Moore—the Lady Be Good gunner who accompanied Sergeants Ripslinger and Shelly into the towering sand dunes in a last-ditch effort to find water and help—are found and borne home to his final resting place.

Dennis E. McClendon
Lt. Col. USAF (Ret.)
Tampa, Florida
July 1982

I returned, and saw under the sun, that the race is not to the swift, nor the battle to the strong, neither yet bread to the wise, nor riches to men of understanding, nor yet favour to men of skill, but time and chance happeneth to them all.

—Ecclesiastes, 9:11

The magnificent stained glass window memorializing the Lady Be Good and its crew and bearing the legend, "IN MEMORY OF NINE WHO MADE THE DESERT A HIGHWAY FOR OUR GOD, ANNO DOMINI 1943. LORD GUARD AND GUIDE THE MEN WHO FLY." The window was taken from the chapel at Wheelus Air Base, Tripoli, and reassembled in the Air Force Museum as the centerpiece of an exhibit featuring the work of U.S. Air Force Chaplains.